WHY MARRY A MAN YOU DON'T NEED?

Nicole

Enjoy your Journey!

WHY MARRY A MAN YOU DON'T NEED?

A Candid Conversation About Marriage, Money, Success, and the Black Woman

CARMEN HOPE THOMAS

FUTURE FAMILY PUBLISHING
Huntsville, Alabama

Why Marry a Man You Don't Need?

A Candid Conversation About Marriage, Money, Success, and the Black Woman

By Carmen Hope Thomas

©2015 Future Family Publishing

ISBN (Paperback): 978-0-9984447-0-3
ISBN (Hardcover): 978-0-9984447-2-7
ISBN (eBook): 978-0-9984447-1-0

Scriptures noted are taken from the following Bible versions:

King James Version Bible

Future Family Publishing
161 Nick Fitcheard Road NW
Huntsville, AL 35806
www.futurefamilypublishing.com
(650) 822-7636

Contents

Acknowledgements   vii

Dedication   ix

Preface   xi

Foreword   xv

Introduction   xviii

Special Note From the Author   xxxiv

1. The Man I Didn't Need   1

2. The Stats   15

3. The African American Female Situation   30

4. Stop Lying to Yourself, Please!   46

5. Single Mama Drama   56

6. What is a Wife?   64

7. That Guy You Never Called Back   85

8. WANTED: A Healthy Black Family   92

9. A Currency Called Intimacy   101

10. A Woman is Only a Woman When She Allows   113
     Her Man to be the Man

11. Sistas Doin' it for Themselves   118

12. This Whole Thing About Love and Respect   130

13. Where to Go From Here   134

     About the Author   138
     Quotes Database   141
     Citations   144

Acknowledgements

I must acknowledge my late mother, Carol Yvonne Williams. My mother was the smartest, most intuitive female on the planet. She learned the hard way some amazing truths about relationships, and she wasn't stingy with her revelations.

I also must thank my husband—Jason S. Thomas. You are wonderful and amazingly supportive. My sons, JST 1 and JST 2—you guys are my heart! You are the reason why I wrote this book—to hopefully inspire a new generation of women for you to choose from.

My sisters, Karen Hope Jones and Andrea Hope Samuel—HA! Thanks for being my ears. You guys are great, and our Saturday morning conversations with Pop are the highlight of my week. What would I do without you—no clue!

To my little Sis, Nikki Thomas and my good girlfriends, Teena Riley, Sharon Riley, Dr. Helen Powell Stoddart, Natasha Johnson Gregg, Nichola Baker, Chantal Livitchi—you have all inspired me in some way to do this without even knowing.

To my Pop, Cleveland Williams, I want to thank you. You do

things that you don't have to—and for that I thank you. You are the kind of parent who is there but knows just how to influence a decision without taking away our ability of figuring out the best solution when challenges arise. Thank you.

*For the daughters my
sons will marry...*

Preface

A person who knows their purpose is a satisfied individual. They are happy, and they are helpful.

Have you ever asked yourself, "Why?" Why are you single? Or maybe this is a better question: "What is it about men that is making it so difficult for me to find one who will allow me to be the best woman that I can be—all while giving me the desire to empower him to be the best that he can be?" What is it that you think about men that hinders you from finding yourself in a positive relationship with one? This book will challenge you to think about your personal journey thus far and give you tools that will help you to understand that we all hold the keys to loving healthy relationships. Once we understand that our challenges are shaped by our thinking, what we have been taught and what we have accepted as fact, we can better understand why we have settled into what seems to be a never-ending pattern of bad behavior and poor choices.

Simply put, there are physical reasons why we choose how we choose—and I don't mean physical in the sense of liking men who have broad shoulders and big feet! I mean physical reasons that begin in the brain. How women think and how women were created has been researched and documented as profoundly different from that of men. When you understand that there are not only physical differences, then you can wrap your brain around the psychological differences and make choices that are different from those you are currently making.

Our psychological hang-ups will expose the very essence of what we believe about ourselves and about men. What we have been taught and what we have experienced often makes it very difficult to change patterns of behavior because you can't seem to allow yourself to change direction for fear of pain or loss. Patterns have kept many African American women from ever considering dating or marrying Caucasian, Asian or Latino men. Patterns of behavior have enabled many women to divorce and marry different men with the exact same traits. Patterns are the main reason why many women have given up on dating and marrying because they have come to accept the lie that "All men are dogs" or "All the good men are gay" or "There are no good men" and the list can go on. There are psychological patterns that will continue to shape our decision-making until we choose to interrupt that pattern.

Once we come to understand our psychological condition, then we can come to a spiritual awakening. Often, we try and use the Bible and spiritual teaching as a bandage over an open, infected wound and then we wonder, "Where is God?" in my healing. What I would like to help you to understand is this: you will better understand the teachings of God once you understand how you were created. We are "fearfully and wonderfully" made, and it is no wonder Dr. John Gray wrote the book *Men are from Mars—Women are from Venus* to help couples better communicate. God made us a certain way, and there is no amount of counseling or prayer that will change that. You see, we often pray for the wrong things. We pray for God to change His creation to help us to find something that He never intended for us to have. That very prayer is contradicting the desire of God to give to us what He wants so much for us to have—happy, healthy relationships.

After we have come to some spiritual conclusions, then we can begin to talk about money. "What money?" you may ask. Your money that you make in your career. The money that you value much more than you realize. Successful women in careers aren't as successful in marriage.

Nika C. Beamon, author of I Didn't Work This Hard Just to Get Married: Successful Single Black Women Speak Out really opens the conversation about the single sista's life in a way that would make you long for the days of Kahdesha and Regine in the weekly 90s sitcom, *Living Single* 1

I love the way Nika chronicles story after story of single African American women who defy the odds in their careers and really reach high heights in all areas and I applaud it all... except, I can't help but to think that some of those women still want to be married.

I have a slightly different argument that I would like to share with you that will hopefully help you to see that our perspective regarding our career success and our personal relationships could have a lot to do with where we are in life, whether we choose to be or not.

Some would say, "You just can't have it all!" I say, "Yes you can!" We *can* be successful and married once we define our career success in the context of a God ordained marriage. Then you can use your skills and talents – not just for you or the company you work for, but also for your husband and children, creating an amazing legacy for generations to come.

Foreword

Carmen Hope Thomas is a successful woman—successful as a wife and mother and in business and life. She is the epitome of what a woman should be according to Proverbs 31, industrious, informed, and in charge. She gently commands her environment to allow all the pieces of the erratic puzzle of life to fall into place using God's wisdom. She is certainly a woman to notice.

Carmen and I met several years ago. Interestingly, she knew my family first because they traveled in the same musical circles. I had heard her incredible voice many times but was never able to formally make her acquaintance. Before meeting Carmen, I had not met anyone that does as much as I do or had as much energy as I had. We were baffled by how long it took us to finally meet, but we became instant friends.

Carmen is incredibly enthusiastic about life. She always has a plan and always works to ensure her plans' success. She knows that failing to plan is a plan to fail. Her new book, Why Marry A Man You Don't Need, allows us to glimpse this secret plan and chronicles her journey and the influences that have shaped her thoughts, feelings, and life.

She incorporates old and revolutionary ideas on becoming a woman and marrying a man because of love, appreciation, and respect rather than what he can "do" for you. She wittily declares that being a resolute, strong women means raising and nurturing strong men for the kingdom to allow them to reach their full potential.

You are one of them. You are a strong woman. Maybe you need some fresh ideas or remakes of old ones to draw yourself away from the mundane subjections of life. These concepts will allow you to spring into new awareness of how self-sufficient, strong women can contribute to our communities with the men God has ordained them to partner with. It is erroneous to think that the choices we make to forego incredible, suitable relationships replace the strength of the home.

In her simple, easy to understand language, Carmen humorously teaches us how to stand up to the challenges that thwart our plans and face them head on. In *Why Marry a Man You Don't Need*, she challenges our beliefs and disinformation about the importance of strengthening the family and positively affecting our communities. Carmen Hope Thomas displaces our posterior thoughts and gives us a witty yet insightful way to transform our lives and that of our men from good to great. This book is an amazing find, an incredible story, and a must read. You are in for a treat!

Helen Powell-Stoddart, MD, MS
Physician/Owner
Pain 2 Wellness Healthcare

She opens her mouth with wisdom,
and the teaching of kindness is on
her tongue.
-Proverbs 31: 26

Introduction

I was born in a little town called Ocala, Florida. Ocala is an interesting place for me. I never felt as if I belonged there, but I so loved every street and every neighborhood. It's a lovely town with lots of horse farms and gorgeous weather. The people are friendly, but there was an incredible income gap between those who had and those who had not during the 1970s when I was growing up there. My mom used to drive through some of the lovely neighborhoods on the east side of town. Beautiful homes that I could only imagine living in. My mom even sent me to school on the east side of town, which further made me long for the opportunity to live someplace other than where I grew up. What's funny is, we weren't considered poor. My mom, dad, sisters Karen and Andrea, and I lived in a nice home on eleven acres of land. Living was simple and sweet. We weren't rich, but we were blessed.

What we lacked, in my opinion, was access. You see, we were so close to the community of my mom's poor childhood that we struggled to escape it. We wanted more and we got more, but the reminder of where she came from wasn't that far away. My mom wanted more for the three of us... and I wanted even more for me. Maybe leaving Ocala was the only way I felt I could achieve that,

I don't know. There are days that I long for the simplicity of that life, though. Maybe I will someday go back there again.

When we moved to Gainesville, my mom and dad had been divorced for about two years. I started high school in Gainesville and because I didn't have any friends from grade school there with me, it took me a while to make friends. Although I missed Ocala, I think I was glad to go someplace else. I was okay starting over.

Ocala felt to be a place where most of my friends and family didn't know and didn't want to know anyplace beyond the city limits. No one seemed to want more. There were no trips to New York or vacations to the Caribbean. Everyone was just okay right there, and that seem to bother me. Gainesville was better. Folks there were a bit more exposed. When I think about that time in my life I realize that I was trying so hard to not be defined by what I saw as the limited vision of life in the mid 1970s.

I wanted to marry and have kids, but what I saw as a happy marriage, I couldn't find in my experience of Ocala or Gainesville. There was no one I remember from that time in my life who had one. No one. Now, I am sure they existed, but for me, I didn't see them. There were no couples I was around who inspired me. There were married people who hated each other. There were married people who tolerated each other. There were baby mamas and baby daddies, there were single people with foster children, there were alone people who were just alone... but there was no one who was happily married with happy kids I could look to for inspiration. Now I am sure there will be some who will take issue with my vantage point, but keep in mind, I was about eleven years old at the time, so say what you will—it was MY experience.

So, before all the folks from the old neighborhood start calling—please, hear me out. I am sure there were happily married folks in my neighborhood or in my church, but understand, I was a child living in a very unhappy world and it was hard to see happiness when you are not quite sure what it looks like.

This was my experience, and because of this, for a very long time I have always been conscious of the family dynamic. I think I decided very early which side I wanted to be on. My mother and father didn't make it. Like in most situations of their time, my mom—who was really poor growing up in a large family, struggled for a way out of it all and found it in my dad—who wasn't quite ready to marry.

My mom compromised, and for twenty years there was more unhappiness than happiness. Daddy just didn't feel responsible for my mom's unhappiness or his. I first realized this when I was twelve years old. I remember it now as if it were yesterday. My dad came in to my room and tried to explain that he was leaving. This two-and-a-half minute discussion was my first introduction to how nothing is worth salvaging when two people are so incredibly unhappy.

My two older sisters were already gone, so my mom and I struggled for years. Mom eventually determined that she didn't want to let my dad be her only experience in a relationship. She wasn't jaded by the notion, so she was open to dating again. As time went on, I never realized until now that my mom taught me how to date men from that moment until now. My mom realized that she had far more power than she ever knew, and she used it with wisdom and grace. Once she determined what her ideal man did not look like, she was brave enough and honest enough to not go there again.

My mom dated men for about four years after her divorce from Daddy. Never did she stay out all night. There was never anyone who stayed over to our house, and I never saw her do anything that could have been viewed as compromising. She was a lady. Mommy was charming and intriguing. Never did she flirt suggestively, and never did she appear dumb or clueless. She was no nonsense, classic and beautiful. When I would look at her and her date (oh yes, she took us with her on dates) you could see in his eyes that he was interested. When Mom married my stepdad, there was a stark difference between him and my dad. My Pop (as I call him) respected my dad for who he was and would scold me if I talked bad about him. He never tried to take his place, but he was distinctively different and loving. My mom learned. There was no need for too many do-overs. She got it right the second time.

Mom always reminded me that there are tons of women who would do anything for a man, but men only noticed the ones with standards. I held onto that little nugget for years. I learned quickly to separate myself from all the other women out there. Having some standards is the best way to do that. There was always a list of things that I made clear that I wouldn't do. There was no need to because I learned that not every failure was a failure at all. Some things that didn't come out the way you planned were not for the purpose that you perceived. Pageants were the tools that taught me that.

My first pageant was in 1988. I was in high school, and my mom convinced me to try out for the Miss Gainesville Pageant. I didn't see myself as the pageant type. I played volleyball and softball. I sang in the school chorus, and I rarely hung out with my friends. I didn't have a boyfriend, and I just wasn't terribly interested in being in a pageant. Being that I didn't have a boyfriend and playing sports didn't make me the most feminine at the time, I always assumed that my mom was trying to help me to grow into my femininity, but that wasn't it at all.

The pageants taught me more about women than they taught me about myself. Girls can be ruthless, mean, hateful, and desperate. It's that sense of hopeless, standard-less desperation that I learned from being in pageants. There were always three types of girls that you meet in pageants. First, the pre-Madonna. That one girl that is just flat out pretty enough to win. She has the hair, the body, and the smile. She is not necessarily the smartest, but she has concluded that she doesn't have to be.

Then, there is the girl who's from the well-connected family and she feels that she is entitled to win just because of who she is. She had dance lessons and voice lessons, and every lesson her daddy could buy to prepare her for her pageant moment. Then, there was me. Girls like me who have natural talent that comes effortlessly and just happened to be there at the right time. Girls who you can't deny are just a cut above the rest. The desperation isn't seen on their face. They are there to light up the stage—take it or leave it—and they are truly a breath of fresh air. You don't know why, but you just like them and you are inwardly rooting for them.

The pageant was held on a Saturday night. I had been practicing on Tuesday nights with the pageant coordinator because the regular pageant rehearsals were Saturday mornings at 10 a.m., and I was always in church at that time. My mom and I had established the standard before signing up. No matter what—I would be in church Sabbath morning. If that couldn't be worked out, I just wouldn't do it. It was because of this decision that I never met the other girls in the pageant until the night of the actual performance. I knew none of them. There wasn't one girl that I ever saw at school, at a game or even at the supermarket. So, when I won, everyone cried "Foul!"

I was the last girl in the talent competition and the others were preparing backstage for the highlight of the night—the evening gown segment. I had done very well during the talent competition and everyone could see that I was a force to be reckoned with. While I was on stage, some of the girls took my evening gown and hid it. Now, anyone that knows anything about pageants will tell you there is probably two-and-one-half minutes between scenes for hair, makeup and wardrobe changes and we couldn't find my dress. The pageant coordinators and my mom were all over the backstage looking for that dress. They finally found it mysteriously shoved in a janitor's closet between a mop and a bucket.

While riding home in the car, my mom told me that I could learn a lot from pageants. "Pageants have more in common with life than any other thing you are doing now. There are those who cheat to win. There are those who win because they just have invested time and money preparing to win and then there are those who are just gifted. That's what you are Carmen, gifted. You needed to see for yourself that you are. Never take it personally when folks don't see your gifts because you may not be the most gifted that time. You must compete because life is a competition. Everyone can't win," Mom told me as she encouraged me to go on.

After winning Miss Florida in the Hal Jackson's Talented Teen Pageant, I graduated high school and was headed off to New York to the Internationals. I had never been to the Apollo Theatre before. I was excited, and I felt like I was on a roll! There were girls there from all over the world, and I was determined to go all the way.

I didn't know it was my turn to understand that I wasn't the best choice. It was difficult, but I got it. Through that experience, my mother taught me that we as women want to believe that we will ALWAYS prevail when we put our minds to something. Whether it's a job, a relationship or a calling... and that's a good thing, but we must leave room for God to expose us to what's best for our ultimate destination in life—which we can't see.

I lost. I didn't even place as a runner-up. My mom tried to encourage me to just enjoy the experience. Take it for what it was and nothing more. Don't take it personally because you didn't win; not everyone will win. I was so disappointed at the time that I didn't even hear her, but I listened. As we got into the car to drive back to Florida, my mom detoured off the route and headed straight to Huntsville, Alabama. Before I could even get too comfortable, my mom was dropping me off to college. Mom had a way of letting me see that there were so many other things to accomplish so get up, stop sulking and get on with it! I realize that is my attitude about everything now. Instead of going on and on about losing, just go on to the next. Instead of going on and on about this guy that didn't work out—count your blessings that it wasn't too serious and that you can move on.

It wasn't until 1992 that I realized that all my pageant experience prepared me for one experience that I could have never planned for... the Miss Collegiate African American Pageant. I was a junior at Oakwood University (then College) and they needed someone to represent the school at the Nationals in Orlando. Oakwood didn't have a campus queen. There was no one to represent the school. The prize was $25,000 to the school and $10,000 to the winner, plus a car, makeup and jewelry. Oakwood didn't have a formal pageant, so the Student Government just voted that I go, and so I did.

All the campus queens from every HBCU were there. No one seemed to know where Oakwood was. While sitting at the airport waiting for our connection to Orlando, the other queens began to recognize that we were all getting on the same flight. I began to mingle, and it didn't take long for me to recognize the three types of women in a pageant. I quickly began to size up the competition, and I established my standards quickly. I even adopted new ones for that specific event just so there would be no confusion about who I was and what I stood for.

Since Oakwood was a vegetarian campus, I made sure that I would be a vegetarian for the two weeks that I was there. As a Seventh Day Adventist, I needed to make sure that the Sabbath was not an issue. To me, I knew that evangelism was the furthest thing from anyone's mind, so I decided to just slip off the radar on Sabbath mornings. No need to make any statements... those people wouldn't care. Lastly, I needed to be modest and pretty. That way, no one at the school could say that I misrepresented them. You see, at Oakwood, we got in trouble for wearing jewelry or dressing immodestly. It made no sense to get on National Television looking like Jezebel's cousin! I set my standards right then.

I have always done the same thing when it comes to men. As soon as you meet a man you need to draw the lines in your mind... no need to make any declarations or announcements. Just do it. People look at what you do and not what you say anyway. Also, people, especially men, find you more intriguing when you are not announcing who you are, anyway. They can discover who you are from their experience with you as they watch how you interact with them and others.

It wasn't long before I saw her. Her name was Rosalind White, and she was from Howard University. I met her in the airport before we even made it to Orlando. I could tell she was sizing up the other girls just like I was. She was there to win, and she was the one to beat. I discovered that most women are never paying attention to what's really important. We sometimes don't take the time to check out our surroundings and the people who are there with us. We are too busy having fun or showing off. I learned from the other pageants that I had previously been in that most of the ladies quickly forget the reason they are there. They forget about the cameras, the prize, they even fail to realize that the judges are at the Meet and Greet watching the ladies and seeing how they act when they don't realize that they are being watched.

Rosalind ended up winning the pageant. I was the first runner-up, and I remember standing on stage once she was crowned to take photos. Everyone was looking for a reaction from me about her winning. The pageant was close. I had photographers and just random people whispering to me, "You should have won." At that very moment, I couldn't react. I couldn't show my emotion because for me it made no sense to at the time. That moment was such a teachable moment for me. How we react to disappointment shapes how we are perceived and who we are.

While standing there, smiling on the outside, I was screaming on the inside and then Rosalind whispered, "Oh my goodness, I just won a car..."—I felt like she was rubbing it in. My first reaction was to tell her I already owned a car or something quick-tongued or sharp-witted to make myself feel better but then my eyes caught a glimpse of my mom. She was standing there, proud and beautiful. I realized in that moment, saying anything wasn't necessary. I had left it all on the stage... it was my very best performance, and the decision was made. When disappointed with defeat, we can often be quick to look for that perfect moment to share a piece of our mind! That bit of sarcasm or a good sharp-tongued put-down! Anything that would inflict pain and deflect our hurt of disappointment. A witty cut-down isn't always the best comeback, especially when silence is an option. It was then that I learned that the same lessons there can be applied in relationships. All my relationships are a string of experiences designed to mold and prepare me for that one moment in time when I would be joined with the right man. Just like in pageants, often it's the timing and your preparedness that determines the outcome. Some would argue the competition plays a role as well but not as much as we think. We are compared to each other as women, but we must not allow our comparison to determine our reaction to one another. Rosalind was crazy talented, beautiful, and prepared. So was I... but only one of us could win. I could have won, and there would have been folks looking at her saying she should have won. In the same way, there are women who end up with certain men and we feel "that should've been me." We can't live our lives replacing other women and their situations with ourselves—expecting the outcome to be the same. It doesn't work that way.

Years have come and gone, and I keep up with Rosalind on Facebook. She lives in the Northeast and is still singing and performing. I honestly haven't seen her since we left Orlando all those years ago. We aren't friends, but I believe there are no bad feelings between us. That experience gave me so many life lessons that I will never forget. The one that I hold closest is a constant reminder, there can only be one queen. If you are not crowned queen, don't take it personally... it's just not your kingdom. Move on, so you can sit on the throne that belongs to you, not someone else.

After college, I felt compelled to succeed. I had done all these great things. I had been in five pageants, three of which I won titles; I was very popular in college, I sang in Dynamic Praise, which was a world-renowned gospel group. I was even voted most likely to succeed by my peers in the choir, so I was under a lot of pressure to measure up to the expectations of others.

I had goals. I wanted to succeed in my career. My degree was in communications: Radio/TV/Film and I dabbled in all of it. My first job was in radio. I was a program director at a little AM Gospel station in Gainesville, my hometown. The station was small. You could barely hear it five miles away, but I worked hard at making this station great. Unfortunately, the owner of the station, Martin, had a wife, Joyce, who wasn't very supportive of me and my creative genius.

The station lacked organization or structure. People came to work late; the music wasn't organized—therefore, everyone played what they wanted. The station had no relationships with record labels or artists and, therefore, we were overlooked anytime anyone came to town.

I made efforts to organize the music, created a structure that gave the employees a little pride and before long, WWLO was a station that people in the community recognized. For a while, I couldn't understand why my boss wasn't so eager for the station to grow. She managed the books for the station and another radio station that they owned that was an FM signal. Of course, the FM was a bit more popular and it made much more money. Most of the time, it seemed the owners didn't care what I did at the AM station, so I put my heart into it. Every once in a while, when the station got a little praise, I never got a pat on the back or any congratulations for my work; the owners took all the credit.

When the local paper wrote an article about me and my role in the success of the station my second year there, that's when I could see that I wasn't being appreciated. You see, for the first time in the history of the station, we had ratings... positive ratings! Often in our lives, no matter where we are, if it's work, relationships or even at church, when we put our heart and soul in it and we are not appreciated, we are faced with an opportunity to define a moment... our moment and our role in that moment. It's hard to not be appreciated. I thought of quitting. I even considered a few choice words to share with my boss and his wife, but I didn't. It's too easy as women to sharpen our tongues with words that pierce. Always being at the ready to give a person a piece of your mind causes you to not think and frankly, it's exhausting!

I decided the high road is the only road I wanted to travel. I worked over two years before I decided to leave and move on. When I look back at those days now, I am glad I did what I did. I am proud of what I accomplished, and I don't even mind that my boss never gave me even a congratulation.

I headed to a TV station in Tampa. Tampa was a very interesting town. I got a job at Channel 38, which ran The Fox Kids Network and a string of reruns and B-list shows. My boss was a young woman named Jane. Jane was never neat. Sometimes she would bring her kids to work with her, and I never knew her husband to have a job. You can tell they had a unique arrangement. One day, I realized that my prospects of moving up were going to be slim. Jane all but made it clear that she was not in favor of me advancing.

I was the only one in my department with a degree and experience beyond that one station. How is it possible that I couldn't move up? I concluded that God had something better for me, and although Jane was trying to block me, God was trying to prosper me. I stepped out on faith, and I left with no backup job in sight. I looked at my goals (yes they were written down), and I realized that I needed to get back on track. I had planned to own a home by the age of twenty-five, and I only had two years at that point to get it in gear.

I moved back to Gainesville and back to radio. I realized that the money was not in on-air work, but in sales. I went to a station that needed a sales staff. WTMG, a hip hop/Urban AC station was where I ended up. I was on fire, and in my first year I doubled my salary that I had from the previous TV station in Tampa, and by my second year, I had my down payment on a home. I was on my way.

I bought my dream car and I was balling, so I thought. I was happy with my career at the point, but dating seemed to take a backseat to everything because most guys at that time were still trying to find themselves. Most brothers were either trying to finish school or trying to get a job. Buying a home at twenty-five years old, for most men, any man, was so far from what they wanted for themselves.

Having a booming career and a home so young made it very hard to date. There were no guys who wanted to date me seriously because it seemed the expectations were just too high. That's when I met Jim... he was ten years older than I, and he was white. I had never dated a white guy before, and I can't say it was terrible. I realized that I needed to be open. So many of my peers would say, "I will never date outside of my race." I didn't want to make such a declaration because I didn't want to be close-minded to anything. God could have had something for me to learn through that experience... and He did. I learned a lot about myself, and I became even clearer about what I wanted for myself. Being open is important. If we truly believe that God knows the beginning from the end, how can we operate from a sense of defined boundaries of where we are willing to go? Sure, have standards but be willing to allow God to show you things about yourself to help you to ever improve.

Jim and I didn't make it, but we have remained friends—even to this day. I continued on my upward tract, trying to get to the next goal... to be a six-figure income earner by thirty years old. Well, I realized I couldn't do it at my present job. I had to go to a bigger market because Gainesville was too small for me to command that kind of salary. So, I put my resume together and I applied in Miami and Atlanta. Now just about this time, I started going out with a guy who lived in Boynton Beach, FL, about forty minutes north of Miami. Also, this was a few months after running into Jason Thomas—an old friend from Oakwood College—at my college reunion. Jason lived in London, so I never thought that we had a chance of anything coming together for us because he lived in another country. Ron, the guy in Boynton, was where my attention was at that moment, anyway.

Ron lived with his mom, and he had a little girl. Not the most appealing, but I was open and as long as my standards remained in place, I was cool. I got both jobs, the one in Atlanta and the one in Miami, but I chose to move to Miami. Miami was about an hour from Ron, which I thought was a good thing. We broke up immediately upon my arrival. Now, some people would have considered that a sign. Perhaps I shouldn't have moved or maybe I should have chosen Atlanta. For me, when you are being prayerful and connected to God, you can still see His leading through the confusing signals of what appeared to be failures.

I got down to Miami and I hit the ground running. Literally! Within a year or so, I was building a home and doing my thing. I took my European vacation about this time, linked up with Jason and later that year he moved to Miami and we started dating there. Jason would have never moved to Gainesville, not from London. So, it was ordered by God that I go there. It makes so much sense now when I look back but then it was not so clear. We have had our ups and downs, but now that we have been married for almost ten years, I can see how all my successes have helped make me into a great wife for my husband. We are a true team... and that feels really good.

Special Note From the Author

For many of my single years, I wrote my thoughts and my feelings in a journal. My pain during my struggles was always tied to what I considered to be losses at the time. Often, when I look back at my journal entries, I realize that what I thought were losses were actually wins. You can't see from what point God has brought you if you never think about where you have been. Journaling is a valuable way of chronicling all the triumphs that might otherwise slip our minds. This is why I have decided to create a special journal, just for you, to accompany you on your journey.

So, go ahead; write, my dear sister. Tell the Lord (and you) whatever you want. Start being painfully honest with yourself and never compromise. Your transformation will begin the moment you open your heart and write.

Please be sure to purchase your new inspirational journal, which, with God's help, will gather your daily thoughts, dreams, and aspirations to bolster your strength as you become the woman you desire to be! You can do it. I believe in you!

Get your journal at: www.carmenhopethomas.com

1

The Man I Didn't Need

I have to tell you about the man that I eventually married. Why am I telling you this? Because I need you to know that I know where you are and how you feel as a successful single woman. It is so easy to huddle on your balcony overlooking your amazing view with a bottle of wine and your toy poodle with hurt feelings wondering why you struggle in relationships, all while comforting yourself with your goal of retiring before you turn forty-five. You don't have to convince yourself that marriage is the tradeoff for being successful because it is not.

Now about this guy named Jason...

It was August 1989, and I had just been dropped off on the Oak-wood College Campus by my Mom and Stepdad with all the normal hugs and well-wishes. There weren't many people on campus because I was early. I had just come straight from New York and the Hal Jacksons Talented Teen Pageant that I had lost. Despite that loss, I was surprisingly upbeat and optimistic about everything in life.

A new campus, tons of potential friends to become acquainted with and all the choirs, clubs and politics to partake in had me geeked. I was determined to see and do it all.

Growing up as a Seventh Day Adventist, I had always gone to public schools. Oakwood was my first Adventist school experience, and I was ready for it. For the first time in my life, I felt like there were other young people who were just like me! I was so eager and naïve about everything, I just assumed there were no obstacles or pitfalls, and I feared nothing!

When I walked into my room, I organized my things and realized my roommate had already checked in. Before even getting a chance to meet her, I had a check that my mom had left me that I had to cash. My folks were eager to get back on the road after they dropped me off so there was no way to get cash because it was after banking hours. With no ATM's back then, I was stuck. I had to go to a grocery store to get my check cashed. I ran down to the lobby and asked a Resident Assistant where I could go to get a check cashed.

"Food World," she said. "Okay," I said, "and where is that."

After a brief set of directions that seem straight forward and easy, yet foreign, I asked her if she had any suggestions on how to get there.

Her blank stare let me know I was on my own.

"Well, Lord," I said to myself, "I am going out here and I am going to find somebody to take me to Food World. With check in hand, my ID and a little money, I walked out of the dorm and headed toward the people all standing in front of the gym.

"Somebody is about to give me a ride, they just don't know it yet," I whispered to myself.

Right by the steps of the gym were two guys and a red Jeep. One guy—fair skinned and the other dark, were standing there looking nice, fine and ready to take me to the store. I walked up to them and introduced myself.

"Thanks for waiting guys, but I am ready whenever you are..." my introduction began, "do you want me to ride in the front or the back?"

They both looked at each other and then looked at me, both seemingly unamused. "Look, I just need to go to Food World to cash a check and then in no time you guys can be right back here in this spot, so if we go now, you won't even realize you were gone. What do you say?" I continued.

"What's your name?" the fair-skinned one asked.

"Carmen... Carmen Hope," I said.

"Now what makes you think that I want to be the one taking you to Food World?" he said.

"Because I am nice and I need to go," I said—flirting, of course.

The dark-skinned guy didn't say much, but he was listening.

It wasn't long before we were off. "Hi, I am Jason," the dark-skinned guy said, "and this is my partner, Donzel."

Donzel was driving during the introduction, and he looked in the rearview mirror and said, "Listen, we are nice guys, but don't ever hop into a car with two guys you just met. Not all guys are nice like us, okay?"

"Okay," I thought, a little surprised but realizing he was right.

When we returned to campus, they dropped me off at my dorm and I can't remember the next time I saw those guys again.

I did remember Jason, though. It was about two years later. Jason and I were coming out of the library and he asked me how I was doing. After some small chitchat, he went his way and I went mine.

Then one day, junior year, I was on campus and I saw Jason again. By this time, I had my own car and I lived off campus. This time, I was giving him a ride. He asked me to give him a ride home. He lived with his parents. I took him to a very nice neighborhood, and he invited me in.

I remember admiring the décor and the dining table. I stayed in the dining room while he went to his room to get his things. When he came out, I remember thinking that he looked like my dad. When we got out to the car, I looked at his hands. I remember his hands very well. He had very long fingers and smooth dark skin.

After I dropped him off back on campus, I would see him every now and again. We weren't close at all, but we would chat here and there.

In 1998, long after graduation, I went back to my college reunion. My girlfriend, Gigi, and I drove up from Florida. Gigi was a good friend who was recently divorced and thought she would roll along with me for the opportunity to connect with her ex-husband (LONG STORY that requires its own book). So, anyway, Gigi and I enjoyed the Friday and Saturday activities—which comprised of walking around campus, church service—i.e. fashion show on Saturday and then Sunday. On Sunday, which is always Easter Sunday, everyone walks around on campus and sees everybody. There are venders, food trucks, and all kinds of activities. That's the day you really want to wear your best and mix and mingle.

Well, Gigi and I had agreed that we would split up and meet back at the car by noon to get back on the road to Florida so we wouldn't get back so late.

Twelve o'clock came and went—NO Gigi! I was hot! Livid!! I almost left her three times. Then I realized I had to find her. Her mother would kill me if I came back without her, so I went looking. There seemed to be thousands of people there. I looked in the gym, in the snack bar, and all around the track field. I walked to the skating rink and even to the natatorium—no Gigi. Now all along the way, I was seeing old friends here and there. Folks I hadn't seen in years, but I clearly was focused on Gigi, and I was ready to make the seven-hour drive and get it over with.

At that point in my life, I lived alone. I had bought a house the year before. My first house—at twenty-five years old. I worked as an account manager at an Urban AC/ Hip Hop station in Gainesville, FL. I was driven, successful, and alone. Also at that time, it didn't bother me, but I was aware that I needed to be meeting men. I had goals. I wanted to buy my first house at twenty-five. Done! I wanted to make six-figures by thirty, and I was well on my way. Somewhere in there, I knew I needed to find the love of my life, get married and have kids— – all while checking off all the other things on my list.

It was two o'clock, and I still hadn't found Gigi! I was really upset now. I had to leave her! At that point, we would be getting home after 10 p.m.—and I was planning to go to work the next day. Although I was enjoying myself seeing old friends, I had to get going; at that moment, I was between the snack bar and the gym when I decided to leave her. I remember looking behind me and then turning to look in front of me, toward my car when I made the decision to leave. It was then, at that moment, that I turned to my left and standing there was Jason, the dark-skinned guy who, along with his light-skinned friend, gave me a ride to Food World almost ten years earlier.

"Carmen Hope!" he said with such swag!

"Jason Thomas!?" I said with all the flirt I could muster!

It was at that moment I realized God was trying to keep me there on campus for this very moment. I had to reconnect with Jason Thomas!! It was, oh, so obvious. Our eyes were glued to each other. I forgot there was anyone else there. And Gigi... Gigi who? You couldn't drag me from that campus! We stood there and we talked. We were both all smiles... totally engaged and very interested in where each of us were in life.

"This is what I am talking about, Lord," I thought, "this could be my man!"

I remember thinking that. I remembered all the diary entries about what I wanted. I remember all the prayers, too. "No matter where in the world he is, Lord, bring us together," I wrote. It was then that Jason told me he had been living in London for about two years. He reminded me that he was born in England and had simply returned home after school. We walked and talked a bit, and I walked him back to his booth. He was a vendor at the campus village.

For about an hour or so we talked off and on between customers. His mother, father, and sister were there helping him. They all noticed the attention we gave each other, and it was crazy noticeable by everyone who came by that knew us both.

Soon Gigi found me! She claimed she had been looking all over for me. Jason and I exchanged numbers and emails and said goodbye. I thought of him the whole way home.

About a year later, I got a call from Jason. He was going to be in Florida—Gainesville, Florida! I lived in Gainesville!! He was coming to help a friend move into her dorm at the University of Florida. Now, you won't believe this, but I knew the girl. She went to my church. Would you believe I never saw Jason on that trip? Never ever saw him! I had started seeing a guy who lived in Boynton Beach, and I was headed to Boynton for the weekend to see him and never saw Jason. What's interesting is, Jason, after realizing that I was going to miss him in Gainesville, then began driving to West Palm Beach—about fifteen minutes north of Boynton, and we were going to connect in West Palm—but that never happened either.

We never connected—that was always odd to me. One thing that I learned from that moment was that you cannot rush a connection that God has ordained. So many times we are in a rush, and we are so desperate for something to come together, but we have to understand that God sees what we cannot see. We have to allow all the elements to come together first so that the relationship or connection will be right.

That year, some of my friends and I talked about taking a trip to Europe. We were planning to go to London, Rome, and Paris. I started saving my money and getting all the plans together. I mentioned it to Jason on one of our few telephone calls. As the time got closer and closer, I discovered that the other girls in our group weren't properly saving their money for the trip, and I was the only one ready to go.

I wasn't sure how I felt going to a foreign country alone. Jason kept telling me to come. He told me I could stay with him. Unfortunately, that was never something I felt comfortable with. I couldn't go stay with a guy in his house in a foreign land and just be okay with it. To me, that would send the wrong message—and remember, I always set my standards at the onset to avoid confusion. So, I didn't go.

Instead of going to England, I moved to Miami. That was when I got an offer from Miami and Atlanta for work, and I chose Miami to be near the guy that I was dating in Boynton, of course, not knowing that our relationship wouldn't work out. Again, a set-back that I didn't take personally.

It was time to meet more men and to put myself in a position to meet my husband and grow. Gainesville was a small town. There were few resources and even fewer men to meet. So, I moved and I am so glad I did.

Moving to Miami was interesting. I had a ton of male friends, but none of them ever became a friend with benefits! In other words, I made it clear there were no gray areas of understanding with any men. It made life a whole lot easier that way. Oh, there were a few close calls, but nothing ever came of it...Praise God!

The first year I was down there, I talked to Jason a lot. Almost every day there was some form of communication. We would email and call. He was so easy to talk to, but he was in England and I was in Miami. He worked for a Dot Com company, and the company sent him to a conference every year. One year, he came to Washington, DC. He thought that he would take that oppor-tunity to come and visit, so he did. We spent a few days together and then he was off. We were never intimate. Never even kissed. Just hung out and it was fun! Often we choose to live life like it's reality TV. We think that it's okay to be sexually intimate on a whim, or flirtatious and revealing. I caution every woman that I speak with to stop allowing television – a world that we all agree is not real, to establish your standards. You can be friends with a man without sexual intimacy. You can do it!

Later that year, I realized I wanted to go on my European vacation. Jason and I were close friends by now, and I felt a bit more comfortable hanging out with him. So, I planned my vacation. I went to London and Paris with Jason. It was amazing. I had so much fun, but I knew I needed to put a stop to this long-distance relationship.

Something very interesting happened to me... it was at that moment that I realized most women would say (and many of my friends did) that it was crazy to be in a long distant relationship with that much time and distance between two people. And I agreed with them. It's not something that everyone can do, but there were several things that I learned from my experience.

Talking about standards... For Jason and I to be so far apart was a huge benefit for us. Yes, I said benefit! It gave us the time and was worth the attention to really talk and get to know one another. We were forced to write, forced to email and call each other and get to know each other on a level that would allow us to marry later. Of course, I didn't know we would eventually marry at that point so I did the unthinkable. I planned to let him know that I couldn't keep it up. The distance was killing me. It was too expensive. The phone calls, the late nights (there was a five-hour difference) were taking a toll on me physically and economically.

Here is a nugget: most women would have been frustrated with a long-distance relationship. I welcomed it at the time because it forced us to talk and get to know each other. Not being close helps to maximize the talk time and limit opportunities of intimacy. Intimacy too soon clouds judgment, and women especially jump the gun with their feelings and expectations. Distance can be your friend. I always advise to use the distance wisely. If you can't have amazingly deep philosophical conversations that don't revolve around sex and what you would do if you were together, then you have the wrong man anyway. It can be expensive, but a woman with some standards can use it to her advantage.

Tearfully, at the end of my first European vacation with my new best friend, I ended it—at least I attempted to. Jason and I just had a few too many miles between us. We had been close friends for almost two years. After a while, it just got frustrating to be so far apart. He then dropped a bomb of his own on me! He told me his job ended. The company folded, and he was currently unemployed. I felt so bad, but he seemed happy because of our new-found friendship. You see, he planned to take this opportunity to move back to the USA, and he did. About two weeks after I came back to Miami, Jason returned to the United States and he moved to Ft. Lauderdale—which is very close to Miami. We were then able to properly date each other.

What's unique about this time is, I was making a lot of money. Jason was starting over. In England, he had an apartment, a good job, a network—everything. In Miami, I had all those things and all he had was me and a few extended family members. We weren't ready for marriage; we were just getting to know each other in the same city.

Here I was, a six-figure income earner dating a guy who was trying to find a job.

"This is not what I had in mind, Lord!" I thought.

I felt stuck. I had invested all this emotional time and energy with him, and I believed in my heart that he was a great man capable of even greater things. I believed I could be a fabulous support for him. I could be his Michele, and he could be my Barack.

I can look back on it now and see what I couldn't see back then. I felt like I was taking a leap of faith dating Jason at that time because we were so far from each other on the socioeconomic scale. Just to give some perspective, I was building a house and owned a rental property while he lived with a family friend. He was able to get his old car back from college—a Honda Accord—at least fifteen years old at the time—to ride around in, and I had a BMW for work and I drove a Lexus on the weekends to church or to go out. I could have easily said that this wasn't going to work, but I thought and prayed about it. I knew that this man that I got to know so well was capable of more; he just needed a woman to help support him through to it.

So, instead of always going out to eat, I cooked. After every meal, I packed the leftovers and I let him take them home for his lunches the next day. We never lived together. I needed it to be clear that he was taking care of himself and not me taking care of him. I helped create an environment that would help empower him, not enable him, and that was my focus... empowerment. I didn't want him driving my car or living with me. I made it clear that I was cool with where he was, and I didn't pressure him to do anything more than what he was doing.

Within two years, he had bought a small condo on the beach. He opened his own business, and he was doing his thing. We dated still, but now things were different. He realized there were choices, and he dated around. I was cool with that. I dated around too, but my standards never wavered and I was able to say, "It's okay," if this didn't work out.

We dated off and on for about six years after that. I finally said enough is enough. I figured I was getting too old to be in a relationship without a real destination, so I left. I moved to Washington, DC after selling my house. There, I was able to start over. I dated, and I got to know myself better. I had many friends tell me that I had wasted some of my best years on Jason. For me, I couldn't think that way about it. I had to see that it was all a part of the plan. I was smart enough to see that God allowed that relationship for a season to teach me a lot about myself. Within two years, Jason came back to me and asked me to marry him. Within that same year, we were married. Now, almost ten years later, we have two boys and a thriving business and ministry together.

Another nugget: I firmly believe that we as women should create an environment of love and support for any man that we love. He has to know that you will allow him to lead you, and he will be careful where he decides to take you because he respects that you trust him to go. Most women are quick to let their man know that they won't be doing this or won't be doing that—which in most cases will make a man unsure of himself and quick to blame his woman or anyone else when things don't work out the way he planned. Love and unwavering support is what any man needs for a lifelong relationship to last. Did I need to marry Jason? No. I didn't need to marry him or any man. By our society's standards, I was doing my thing! I was making money and my career was great. I married him, though; believing that what we could create together—with him leading the way—was something bigger than anything I could do on my own. The benefits for me were a great partner, two fun kids and an even greater career!

2

The Stats

———————

There are major changes in our society that makes meeting, dating, and marrying a challenge. The traditional values, the traditional methods, the meeting and marrying someone in the same town or village, have vanished from our society in general. Men and women no longer live the same lives as they did fifty years ago, or even twenty-five years ago. Parents no longer introduce their son or daughter to their friend's son or daughter in their teens or early twenties. And on top of this, we have a society where changing partners, sexual brief encounters and divorce have become more acceptable. These practices are only beginning to surface and effect how men and women look at commitment. Work is far more demanding and lives are more transient. Financial stability, companionship or just wanting to be married are no longer reasons why men and women marry.

The substantial rise of successful women has also changed the psychological and romantic outlook for women. Women have swapped their feminine qualities for more masculine energies. Women are more practical, more educated and driven—and they must be in order compete and succeed in an ever-changing male dominated world.

There are more options for women, more practices that were never acceptable before being entertained now, and we will discuss them all in detail. In our discussions, we will ask ourselves some tough questions about our expectations in our lives as women, in our relationships and explore what exactly it is about marriage that we want for ourselves.

"Men are NOT intimidated by successful women; it's a myth perpetuated by WOMEN who think their success and intelligence is the reason they are not in a relationship. But it's actually down to evolutionary programming!" -Jill Rhodes Harvey[2]

Okay, ladies, we women are 50.8 percent of the U.S. population.

Women earn almost sixty percent of undergraduate degrees, and sixty percent of all master's degrees.[3]

Women earn forty-seven percent of all law degrees, and forty-eight percent of all medical degrees.

Women earn more than forty-four percent of master's degrees in business and management, including thirty-seven percent of MBAs.

Women are forty-seven percent of the U.S. labor force, and fifty-nine percent of the college-educated, entry-level workforce.

These Same Women hold almost fifty-two percent of all professional-level jobs. They are 14.6 percent of executive officers, 8.1 percent of top earners, and 4.6 percent of Fortune 500 CEOs. [4]

They hold 16.9 percent of Fortune 500 board seats.[4]

In the financial services industry, they make up 54.2 percent of the labor force, 12.4 percent of executive officers, and 18.3 percent of board directors.

They account for 78.4 percent of the labor force in health care and social assistance, only 14.6 percent of executive officers and 12.4 percent of board directors.[4]

In the legal field, they are 45.4 percent of associates—twenty-five percent of non-equity partners and fifteen percent of equity partners.

In medicine, they comprise 34.3 percent of all physicians and surgeons and 15.9 percent of medical school deans.

In information technology, they hold only nine percent of management positions and account for only fourteen percent of senior management positions at Silicon Valley startups.

Furthermore...

Women control eighty percent of consumer spending in the United States and three percent of creative directors in advertising.[5]

Women accounted for sixteen percent of all the directors, executive producers, producers, writers, cinematographers, and editors who worked on the top-grossing two hundred fifty domestic films of 2013 and were just twenty-eight percent of all off screen talent on broadcast television programs during the 2012-13 prime-time season.

When, however, there are more women behind the camera or at the editor's desk, the representation of women onscreen is better: films written or directed by women consistently feature a higher percentage of female characters with speaking roles.

The point of letting the world know just how amazing you women are:

Women no longer need marriage for financial stability! Women no longer look to marriage for validation or a way to social status. Woman can literally take care of themselves and a few other people as well. The point of highlighting just how amazing you are just proves that you don't need anything in your life to continue to be successful.

Young women who are succeeding in the workplace are finding it difficult to establish relationships with men who are not succeeding in their careers. This dynamic makes marriage an option that is often refused.

Change in Women's Representation in Select Occupations	1970	2006-2010
Registered nurses	97.3%	91.2%
Dental assistants	97.9%	96.3%
Cashiers	84.2%	74.7%
Elementary and middle school teachers	83.9%	79.3%
Pharmacists	12.1%	52.6%
Accountants	24.6%	60.0%
Computer programmers	24.2%	24.4%
Physicians and surgeons	9.7%	32.4%
Lawyers and judges	4.9%	33.4%
Police officers	3.7%	14.8%
Civil engineers	1.3%	12.7%

Let's face it, women have options. They are far more prepared than ever in their careers and their ability to build amazing families. When I think about my journey and of every woman who is close to me, I feel more and more empowered by these women and I am proud of the woman that I have become because of them. What I love about truly strong women is that they don't require their men to be weak for their relationships to work. Neither does their strength need to be managed by an even stronger man. In our society, we seemed to have bought into the notion that strong women equal weak men. Or strong men require their women to be weak and obedient. That thought seems to bolster the image that most people believe. men who are career-minded, educated and well-traveled are not likely to choose man who is a less educated, blue collar homebody! Let's follow the above statistics and assume this for the sake of argument.

Women in the 1970s were only 12.1 percent of the pharmacists, now women are 52.6 percent. In the 1970s, we were only 4.9 percent of the lawyers—now, 33.4 percent. The other side to that story... first time marriages went from seventy percent in the 1970s to right at fifty percent by 2010, and that number is steadily declining. So, what is it about women's career ambitions and their goals as wife and mother that are so difficult to coexist together? What is it about our society that makes it so hard for women to find that balance with career and family? We tend to hold on to our strength to justify its inability to occupy the same space as our men and our children.

Must we always sacrifice our children, our husbands and our relationships for that fantastic career? Are we just typical women who have got to have it all? Is having it all way too much? Perhaps it's not us, as women, but it's our men... is it true that they would prefer that we are at home—barefoot and pregnant? With no ambitions, no goals or thoughts of our own? Frieda Klotz, a contributor for Forbes magazine writes, "The undeniable implication of all this is that being self-sufficient and successful will probably wreck your love life. Hadley Freeman encapsulates the point brilliantly: 'the media loves any story that suggest independent women will be punished and ... many women readers, in my experience, grab on to articles that voice their worst fears.'"[6]

I found this quote to be so interesting. It seemed to go against everything that I was arguing. Often, when talking to women, it's hard to get them to believe that their success is not some sort of punishment for taking a man's place in the world, which requires them to live alone. All areas of society seem to have bought into this notion. I totally reject it.

In 2008, Lori Gottlieb made the case for "Settling for Mr. Good Enough" in Atlantic Magazine. Gottlieb caused a stir by arguing that women's value sinks when she has hit about 35. Even before that there is cause for worry. As Gottlieb revealed, "Every woman I know—no matter how successful and ambitious, how financially and emotionally secure—feels panic, occasionally coupled with desperation, if she hits thirty and finds herself unmarried."[7]

This also comes up in conversation among women who are feeling their clock tick. So often we hear that our standards need to be adjusted or perhaps that we want too much. I refuse to embrace that ideology and know that I am not advocating that line of thinking either. I feel we must address these common questions in order to get to the root of our plight.

Kate Bolick, in an article in the Atlantic, tells how she rejected a series of perfectly nice suitors when she was younger. Now, at thirty-nine, she wonders if she will ever marry. She goes on to argue not only that the institution of marriage is dying, but even more worrying, that because of economic shifts, the "high-status American urban male" is becoming increasingly hard to find.

Bolick tells readers that as women attain parity with men—they are more likely than men to go to college and are (maybe) starting to earn similar amounts—the number of traditionally "marriage-able" men is shrinking. Status is the key term in Bolick's choices.[8]

Fortunately for you, this book has been written to take on the conversation and get us all talking from a different perspective as successful women are increasingly seeing the challenges. Let me empower you with this:

One of the most incredibly powerful individuals in the world is a Black woman who is successful in her career and happily married. –Carmen Hope Thomas. She has the power to literally move mountains, manifest immediate provisions out of thin air...

I believe we have been hoodwinked and bamboozled into resisting the urge to be in a loving relationship because we have been convinced that we must trade it in for our American Express Black Card. Unfortunately, we have all developed an appetite for the forbidden.

Proverbs 9:17 states, "Stolen water is sweet and bread eaten in secret is pleasant." We have had over four hundred years of behavior that has rewired the standards of people of color. Black men have been bred like prize winning horses—coupled with Black women who were expected to produce at least ten offspring each.

In our freedom, we have now—more than ever—enjoyed intellectual power and financial provision. We now recognize some of the reasons that we have kept habits that are detrimental to our own wellbeing—fueling the demise of our families and our communities.

How do we initiate a paradigm shift? We have to recognize that the enemy has completely orchestrated your singleness. Finally, we recognize how the traps have been set, we see how the old views of our community have shaped our current situation as a community.

It's through a new level of consciousness we can—a single, successful Black woman, prepare for what God has for us. A prepared successful Black woman—mentally, emotionally and spiritually, prepared—is a beautiful, happy bride and an amazing wife.

In the April 3, 2015 Hublpages.com article, "Successful Women Don't Attract Husbands, But Why?", author Jill Rhodes Harvey reminds us that our society is more equal than ever before. Women overall have achieved equality in many ways—yet the more educated and successful women are finding it more than challenging to find love and a husband. Finding your soul mate, husband, life partner or love of your life, has become more and more unlikely—especially after thirty-five. There are now more single women over thirty seeking a life partner than in any time in the last century. Some would argue, the history of the world![2]

For the successful professional female over thirty-five, the chances are truly grim but not impossible. We must remember, men and women are genetically programmed to look for partners in our early twenties. If you were anything like me, decision-making was not my strong suit in my early twenties, so all the guys I dated at that time were not marriage material. It's important to note, we must look at the process of dating differently. We must accept the changes in our society and the way things are done, but we don't have to accept the prognosis that is being bounced around in the media as our likely fate.

I married at thirty-six years old. YES! It can happen. Believe me when I tell you I was headed down a lonely spiraling road to 'Single-Dom' when I decided that it was my thinking and my practices that were perpetuating my problem.

Being single over thirty-five is scary. I don't want to belittle the anxiety that comes with that reality, but nowadays, thirty-five is young compared to the expected lifespan most of us can look forward to. It's not just scary for women, men too are facing a more challenging position when ready to find a life partner. Women's roles, approach and ability to be in control of their lives, has changed drastically over the last fifty years. Men and women are no longer on the same path at the same time. The most natural time to pair up is between twenty and twenty-eight because our genome programming makes us most sexually attractive (physically, at this time) and women are their most fertile. In the last fifty years, this has changed. Women no longer see marriage and having a family as a goal anymore, well not until they have almost reached the end of their natural biological capabilities. Men are starting to realize they have a clock as well! No longer can they kick the proverbial marriage can down the road. The fact is: Mother Nature has not changed women's biological clocks and physical peak as in the ease at which to become pregnant has not changed—and neither has it changed for men.

The 1950s and 60s seemed to bring about a sexual awakening for both men and women, which on the surface, women celebrated. Women felt that the home didn't have to be their only destination as it related to their contribution to the family. Women wanted options and education. The feminist movement also created a culture for women who wanted to be seen and treated equal to men, which has had its rewards and its drawbacks. Many women would argue that they don't want to give up their option of working outside the home to have a loving home with a man in it. Where is the happy medium?

As the modern woman has exercised her right to be equal in all ways, meeting genuine eligible men, who she considers her "Professional Equal" feels impossible. Oh, and he has to be emotionally mature, financially more secure than her, stable and ready for marriage! With requirements like that, it's no wonder the number of men has reduced considerably over the years, to the point, that the thirty-five-year-old successful woman who's been focused on her career, enjoying her single life, traveling and becoming financially secure is struggling to find men who look past the casual hook up.[9]

Most successful males are dating. The dating that they are doing is likely to be the casual flings, hook ups, or "Bootie Calls" because they just do not feel compelled to have personal demands matching their professional ones—because we have reprogramed ourselves over the past fifty years to do things differently. Remember, we don't encourage young ladies to even look for love until college is finished. Sometimes college is more than just four years; in many cases its eight to ten. Then we are encouraged to get a good job and discouraged from getting off our career path. When we do meet someone worthy in our younger years, we force ourselves to stave off the desire to commit, waiting for some magic perfect moment to marry and have kids, all while our corporate ladder is still moving ever upward.

Not all, but a greater proportion of men today are not of the mindset to commit. Why? Because women have made it easier for men to look for a woman he can hook up with until he decides to move on to the next. Women have sex far more readily without being in a committed relationship. You may ask, "What so wrong with that? Men have been like that since the beginning of time!" That may be so, but a man who is looking for a wife isn't likely looking for a woman who mimics or acts the same as a man. We must stop perpetuating the problems that both men and women have with committing by "Moving the Goal Post" of our standards. Both men and women, over time, have contributed to the commitment issues that cross racial, ethnic and socioeconomic lines. Everyone is struggling with commitment issues. Online dating sites are a clear indication of our issues.[10] Research has shown that two out of every five males online is already in a relationship, and that's just the ones who have been willing to divulge that information for research purposes.

"The most attractive, accomplished, men and women who seem to have it all, are still finding it challenging to meet Mr. or Ms. Right..." -Jill Rhodes Harvey

In our grandparents time, women and men knew what was expected of them. Men were taught that it was their number one priority to be a provider. Men are wired to be providers, and they wanted the job of being the provider. For women, they were excited about marriage and children. Having a family was everything, but in today's society those expectations are not that strong. Everyone's priorities seem to be fixed on a successful career. It's the introduction of options that appears to weaken the strongest of our desires when it comes to relationships. Priorities, goals and desires—along with our fears, our parents miss steps, and social phobias, all get a little muddy when it comes to deciding what we really want in life.

Even with these distractions, God has programmed men and

women to be attracted to and desire certain elements in the opposite sex, and all the equality in the world won't change that. Women who do not understand this must understand that there are some things that can't change. We must accept these evolutionary facts. Let's examine how and what triggers men's reaction to women, and what men look for, even if subconsciously. Women and men can naturally look after, nurture, provide for a family, but does that mean we should elect to do it without a partner because we are too stubborn or unwilling to go through the emotional process of relationship building?

Where a woman naturally demonstrates softness, warmth, sensitivity, empathy, compassion, a man is programmed to be the hunter, gatherer, nurturer, and pursuer of women; if a woman comes across with masculine energies, the "I can take care of myself, so you better be able to do more than I can" attitude, regardless of how gorgeous looking she is—most men will not be interested in competing with a female love interests for the job of provider of the home. He may even be physically attracted, but most men aren't compelled to pursue her further as a potential wife or mother.

Once we stop trying to rewrite our genetic code and start focusing on ways to be women in our relationships and not competitors, then we can start seeing that men need to be supported and respected by their women.

I've heard from women, " Men are intimidated by me as I'm as driven as they are," but is that true? Could it be that men are not attracted to a woman that is trying to show up every man that shows a little interest in her? Could it be that men are attracted to the parts of a woman that are not like them? The loving, compassionate softness that women can bring to any situations is attractive to a real man, which does not mean she has to be subservient, but she just has an understanding of how men and women who are truly the masculine and feminine opposites of each other naturally fit together like a hand in a glove.

You may not control all the events that happen to you, but you can decide not to be reduced by them.
-Maya Angelou

3

The African American Female Situation

It's no secret that successful Black women struggle to meet and marry equally successful Black men. Even more disturbing are the statistics that Black women face when trying to meet and marry a moderately successful Black man. According to the Journal for Blacks in Higher Education, sixty percent of Black students receiving degrees are women and Black women make up seventy-one percent of graduate students.[11]

Look, my sister, I get it. I have been there, and I have felt the pain. I too wondered was all the time and energy that I put in my career worth it. I remember the day I realized something had to change. I was about thirty-three years old. I worked in advertising and marketing for one of the largest media groups in the country. I made a pretty good income, and I was leaving work early that day to go and close on a new home I was building. I should have been happy, but I wasn't. On my way to the closing, I spoke with my mom and she made a sobering comment.

She said, "Don't put too much stuff on the walls 'cause there aren't too many men willing to live with you in your house!"

"What!" I said. "What does that mean?"

Mom didn't answer, leaving me to assume what she meant that so I would think.

After my closing, I went back to my office for a meeting. As I sat around the conference table, I kept thinking about what my mom had said. As I looked at everyone sitting there, I noticed something. We were all professionals, educated and highly successful. Out of the ten people there, seven women and three men, all the women were unmarried. Two men were married and one man—divorced. All of us were six-figure income earners and that's when it hit me. I was the youngest woman there and as I looked at my boss—a fifty something divorced woman with an ex-husband who ran off and her only son committed suicide before the age of thirty, I wondered if all the money and corporate trips were worth it. I realized that I was headed down the same lonely path, and I decided then that I didn't want to keep going. Already I was struggling to meet and date men who I felt were worthy, but the more successful I became the problem seemed to persist.

I used to believe that the ultimate reward for being a "good girl" was the husband, 2.3 kids, house and the happily ever after. Unfortunately, that is not altogether my story...

I went to college, graduated... bought my first home at twenty-five, was a six-figure income earner by thirty, and I didn't sleep around, had no kids before marriage, I was never 'that girl' in the club—I truly believed in the reward. Unfortunately, my focus seemed to be a little misguided. It wasn't wrong to believe that there is a reward for being good, I just shouldn't have expected it... I believe that God blesses us once we have come to a point in our understanding of the impact of our existence in this world. My blessings came once I stopped expecting to be rewarded and started focusing on the world around me and my place in it. Here's my story:

I was finally getting married. Jason and I had set our date and plans were underway. We decided to go together to our doctors, he to his urologist and I to my gynecologist, for a "before marriage" checkup. Jason checked out okay. After my initial visit, my doctor ordered an immediate follow up. So, I went, and it was there we discovered some issues.

"The chances of you having any children are very slim," my doctor said in a cold, uncaring tone as I sat staring at the floor. "Tell me, why did you wait so long to have kids? Most women your age would have had kids by now." I can't even describe what I felt. It was indignation mixed with fear! The nerve of the doctor to say something so rude—am I wrong for wanting a husband FIRST before making babies? How dare he suggests that it's my fault, and somehow I should have just had some kids in my prime so I could say I got that done. Who cares that I would not have been prepared to give them a loving environment during my fertile prime! I wanted to cry and punch him all at the same time!

My heart sank. I felt destroyed and useless. I couldn't believe it. Jason took me by the hand, and we left. We found another doctor and got another opinion once we got married. I had surgery, and soon we were pregnant. In my late thirties at the time, happily married and pregnant, I soon realized that long gone were the thoughts of making money and setting sales records. No longer did I care about the latest fashion, my focus was growing inside of me.

I know I was not the first to have a baby, nor would I be the last, but there is something amazing about having a baby for a man who loves you enough to "put a ring on it" and is excited about taking care of you and the baby. For the first time in my life, I was in a position to focus on someone other than myself. There were no thoughts of how the bills would be paid, no thoughts of how I would meet this deadline at work, no thoughts of how was I going to do it all... none of that. That's when it hit me. For all the times that I considered trying to do it another way, I was a fool. At one time in my life, I considered my job and my position, the money or the status paramount to everything in my life. Now, none of that mattered to me! This time it was all about my baby, my husband and our lives. I understood at this time of my life why God designed it this way because it was in this environment that I saw things differently. No amount of money could change my situation, so I had to depend on God and Jason.

Perceived status is a distraction. Houses, cars, and Louis Vuitton—distractions! I had no distractions. I was finally paying attention. Every time I felt him kick, every time I looked at myself in the mirror and saw my own mother in my face, I realized that I had a responsibility that was more exciting than any sales goal or bonus check. I could see that I had an opportunity to pour into a little life that could in turn pour into society. Children are so much promise. They can change our neighborhoods, our communities, and our country. Children have an amazing ability to show you yourself and cause you to be more patient and more conscious than you ever thought you were capable of being. Children.

The Position of Power

Here is the point of this entire line of reasoning that I would like to share with you about children who are born in a position of power (that position includes a support system that is loving and represents the man and female dynamic for positive growth). Consider this: while studying my Bible, I tried to imagine myself living in ancient Israel and something occurred to me; every family before the birth of Christ assumed that their son could possibly be the Messiah. They had read about the coming Messiah and taught all their children about Him.

Imagine the power of each household with a son in it. The care they took in what he watched and what he participated in. Imagine the care to properly train him and how they noticed every potential talent and interest he may have had. I surmised, through my own reasoning, that this is possibly where the ritual of the bar mitzvah may have come from.[12] The Bar (בַּר) is a Jewish Babylonian Aramaic word literally meaning "son" (בֵּן), while bat (בַּת) means "daughter" in Hebrew, and mitzvah (מִצְוָה) means "commandment" or "law" (plural: mitzvot). Thus, bar mitzvah and bat mitzvah literally translate to "son of commandment" and "daughter of commandment."

Even in other cultures around the world, sons and daughters are celebrated through all kinds of cultural ceremonies, giving them a commission that the entire community can come together and witness. Ancient and present day African tribes present their sons to the world through a ritual called the "Rite of Passage."[13] The ritual marks the passage from child to adult male, each sub-group in Africa having its customs and expectations that have been chronicled for thousands of years.

One of my most vehement arguments for writing this book is this: as a woman of means... you, my sister, with your education and your successful career are the most qualified to be happily married with children who are raised in the tradition of our ancestors—keeping in mind the desperate need to provide a culturally conscious education, one centered on our traditions and empowerment—instead of having your son for some guy you met at the club!

I believe that we must not allow ourselves to get so self-absorbed into our own agenda and accomplishments that we miss the real need of our community. We have the power to change the direction of who we are as a people and how we have been maligned and mistreated. If we are not given the justice and restitution that we deserve, then we can take it through our well informed and well prepared reinforced family unit. You are the most important piece to it all.

I can't help but think about my journey as a new mother. All I wanted was to do for my children even more than what was done for me. I had the means to do it, just as you have the means to do it. We have to see ourselves as successful women as more qualified to move our families according to the same commandments that a typical Jewish family sees their role. We have the resources and the knowledge to change things in the media, in our schools, and in our communities. We all scream that things should change—well, let's change them. It's easy to ignore a kid that is poor with a mom who is less educated and a dad that is absent. But imagine what life would be, by inserting the power and influence of a two-parent household, with a child in the same environment—having the knowledge of how municipalities work, the knowledge of how communities and schools are funded and the ability to influence policy and change... both children can benefit when we are all thinking our how to benefit all and not just the elite.

You see, in my opinion, the Western "survival of the fittest" mentality doesn't work for the Western culture, and it doesn't work for us as peoples of the African Diaspora. I came to realize that for there to be real change in our community that we must see the changes to benefit as many as possible. I actual think about the girls that my sons will marry, not impregnate.

We have to begin to think about the next generation of who we are in order to truly change things.

One day, I asked my husband this question: "Why did you choose me to marry?"

He said, "There was another girl that I was talking to and then there was you. With her, I could have built a village, but with you, I felt I could build a nation." His response has become the sponsoring theme for this book.

Imagine if we all purposed to build a nation through our relationships. Our focus would change. Our purpose for loving and living will evolve into a God ordain vision for the entire community that you are connected to.

You must understand that it's about more than finding a husband or a wife. It's about more than just having kids. God is looking for us all to want to change the trend of creating families out of the occasional hookup. There were two very distinct covenants that God established in the Garden of Eden, Marriage and the Sabbath. Both of which few regard as sacred anymore. Casual relationships will not change the way our generation perceives family or commitment. Someone must be willing to see the bigger picture and the bigger picture needs to have more than a bunch of young professionals balling and showing off their success with jewelry and flashy things. Somewhere there must be some that are willing to focus on family, on legacy and lineage.

I was thirty-three weeks pregnant when my mother died. I threw up constantly for six hours that night. My heart was heavy, and I couldn't understand why this was happening to me. I had thoughts like, "If I had married sooner, my mom could have seen my kids." I thought, "All that I have tried to be is good, maybe if I had a child earlier, maybe..." All these crazy thoughts that were focused on my loss and pain. No thoughts of legacy or promise.

Then I realized that it is in those moments that the greatness that is within us must show up to get us through it. I had no idea how to bounce back from that grief, and I am still working through it every day; it's far from over, and it's been eight years since she died.

My mother's death is a part of my process for growing and legacy building. All the things that I have ever learned from her seem to magnify once I didn't have her anymore. Now, I can actually hear her voice in my own when I talk to my sons. I can see now that God, although I don't believe that it is His will that any of us should die, but if He should allow that to happen, it is our responsibility to glean all knowledge and truth from our experiences—no matter how painful. Now I know that my life's goal has always been to be a great mom. I didn't know it when I was single and had a successful career, but I know it now.

My mom, her mom and her mother's mom—all are a part of my process. From the moment I felt my eldest son move inside me, I realize that my focus for years was just wrong. I wasn't mature enough to understand it all, but I have had so many more tools to build a fantastic family, plus I have a lineage of women who did it with far less than what I have. The mistake we often make is, we don't see our opportunities as just that, opportunities! We get bogged down in self-promotion and self-denial, and we don't even think about those that are counting on us to move the family and community higher.

As women and as mothers, we have to realize that the responsibility to create environments that are breeding grounds for beauty and growth lies within us! Our homes should be places where our husbands can feel like the king and our kids can feel loved and secure, and we are the ones who make that distinction. The careful balance comes when the demands on your job are presented to be greater than those demands in your home. You have to decide which is greater.

I spoke once for a group in Pensacola, FL. One of the things I shared with them was my fear, as an unmarried successful woman in a career, finding a man with the ability to take care of me in the same way in which I took care of myself. I honestly never ever expected to meet a man who could take care of me, so I found that my expectations were low. When I met men, I was looking for someone to come into my life and help me with the things that I couldn't do for myself, like have kids or do things around my house (notice I said, MY house). What's interesting is that is exactly what I attracted—men who didn't have a home, men who had kids with other women and men who were in school or between jobs. Once I stopped putting myself, what I had accomplished and my need to procreate before the need to have healthy families in my community, I met my husband—who takes care of me and our family.

Place Values

I once heard about a girl in middle school who told her teacher that when she grew up she wanted to have two kids. Her teacher asked her, "Wow, you don't want to get married first?" The girl said, "No! If I marry him, I can't collect child support!" When I heard that story, all I could do was feel sorry. I felt sorry for the damage that this poor child has witnessed. What's interesting is that the thinking is pretty much the same across all socio-economic groups of society. We don't see the immediate value in having meaningful relationships that are built on the foundation of commitment and love. We seemed to be more concerned with making sure that whoever we have our kids for can afford the child support payments instead of making sure we are seeking the kind of connections where our children are brought into the world through relationships that are more important than the children themselves. Our children are wonderful, but they are a product of the relationships that they are born into and when the relationships are broken, then we have a bunch of broken children who then seek other broken children to procreate with and the cycle continues until someone catches on and decides that brokenness is not what they want and therefore make different choices.

My son was six years old when he asked me, "Mummy, why did you bother to marry Daddy? You could have just had me and married someone else?" He said this after his dad scolded him about something bad he had done, but I felt the need to get to the bottom of his comment.

"Why would I marry someone else? I love Daddy!" I said.

"Do you love Daddy more than me?"

"Well, I had to love Daddy for you to come because it's when mommy's and daddy's love each other that God takes that love and makes babies!" I explained, feeling my explanation was superb!

"You don't have to love the daddy to make the baby, though, because my friend Inga doesn't live with her daddy, just her mommy," he said.

"Wait!" I thought. This is not where I wanted to go, but I couldn't turn around now. I was lost for a moment, but I recovered quickly.

I realize that my son sees more examples of single parent households than he sees of two parent households and it is scary. He is a boy and he must see his value in a family or he won't strive to be a father at all—just a daddy, missing in action!

"Son," I explained, "it is my desire to have you, Daddy, and your brother in this family. For Inga, I don't know all the details of her family, but we are a family and I need all of us in it. One day, you will have a family, with a wife and children. That's how God designed the first family and that's how he designed us."

When I looked at my own story, I felt compelled to write a book. Mainly because I have boys who will one day marry. I want them to understand how crucial it is to love when they marry. I need them to know that they must look to build a legacy, and I want them to seek young women who understand that. Our families—no matter what race we look at, are dying. Money, power, self-promotion and politics seems to override the basic goal of family preservation and empowerment.

Don't Believe the Hype

Myths... Lies... "They say" and "I heard"... All kinds of misinformation keep us locked into a never-ending battle with ourselves as to why African American women are not married. There are so many people with theories and "facts" that are far from factual—painting a grim picture of the African American female situation. I know how hard it is. I too was a single woman trying my best to navigate through the minutia to some truth and understanding. Wanting to get married without settling, without having to give it all up or completely give in. Women of color want to have kids, and contrary to the way we are painted in the media, we are not standing down at the Food Stamp line with an EPT test in our hands praying for a positive result just so we can receive some WIC checks and live high off the hog of good ol' Uncle Sam! We are educated, and in a recent study, the most educated group in America. According to the Journal for Blacks in Higher Education, sixty percent of Black students receiving degrees are women and Black women make up seventy-one percent of graduate students.[14]

All my life, I have heard that there are more Black men in prison than in college. If true, this statistic makes it next to impossible to find a husband as an educated Black woman. Fortunately, that statistic is not true. According to the website Blackdemographics.com, 1,034,000 African American men were enrolled in a degree granting institution in 2009 compared to 841,000 who were counted in the nation's jails and prisons during the same year. And of those Black men in jail and prison, only 164,400 are of typical college age (18-24). In fact, even a decade ago when overall numbers suggested there were more Black men in jail than in school, college aged Black men enrolled in a degree granting institution far outnumbered their peers who were incarcerated.[15]

I am sure you have also heard that Black men are more likely to marry white women than Black women. Once again, that is not true. According to Blackdemographics.com, 89 percent of Black men who are married are married to Black women.[15]

Some assume that Black men are gay or players and don't want to be in relationships, but again, that lie is highly overstated and we need to just be honest with ourselves and know that the reason why we are not married or given in marriage is because we don't understand our role, we have had poor examples to look up to and we are just not prepared to be married.

Our history is another factor that must be addressed when understanding why we don't marry. We choose not to marry for so many reasons that are historically woven into our culture and must be faced and acknowledged if we hope to ever reverse our broken past. In many instances, our cultural past has created new patterns of behavior that were forced on flawed factions of our society from racism, single parenting, high rates of divorce over generations and so much more.

Let's stop making assumptions and excuses and start living—looking through different life lenses. Our cultural situation has always been explained by people who don't look like us and care even less about us. We are always getting our story second and third hand. I tell a different story. A story that's positive and true. My story is one of a loving, wonderful husband who is the bread winner in our family. A story that is not filled with drama, no baby mamas or incarceration issues. A story that is more common than the media and even other African Americans are telling. So, stop watching FOX News just long enough to realize that your prospects are better than you think.

I will say it again: a happily married woman can literally change the world! She can make the impossible possible! We have to understand that there is a war against not just us, but the man we are to marry. There is a war against your womb and your unborn children. You must realize that our culture of allowing everything superficial to come before the things that were once held in such high regard, (i.e. marriage, family, home and relationships are what must be addressed).

When you decide that your children and your children's children are more important to you than your job, career or your Michael Kors collections, then we can really talk.

When we begin to want to create a lineage, that if written down in history books and passed along for hundreds of years, that we can be proud of is paramount to anything that we can accomplish on our own as an individual—it's then and only then that our God can share with us the gorgeousness of love with purpose.

Again, stop listening to lies and misinformation. Satan is the Father of Lies. He revels in the thought that we are so focused on nonsense than on what's important. Understand your power and who you are and your role in the overall story of your family and community. Be amazing by being focused on how you can be a prepared successful Black woman—mentally, emotionally, spiritually and how that focus leads you to the beautiful, happy bride and amazing wife you want to be.

I do not wish women to have power of men; but over themselves.
-Mary Wollstonecraft

4

Stop Lying to Yourself, Please!

Before I completely upset you, let me just remind you that I am married and I have two kids. I love my husband, and I know he loves me. My kids are wonderful and we, although not perfect, have been through every kind of struggle you can imagine. We have been broke, and we have both had some serious health issues. Yet, we are still together and we continue to grow in the Grace of God. I needed to say that because I wanted to make sure you knew that I am not going to advise you or instruct you to do anything or believe anything that I haven't come to know for myself. I believe in the Almighty God, and I study and worship with my family, so believe me there will be no 'new age' thoughts or concepts here.

I am writing this book because I was once single and I was fairly successful. I was the accomplished Black woman. I, like many of you, went looking for something and I thought that I knew what it was. I was told to go to college—and I did that. I was told to get a great job, and I did that as well. I was told to buy a home and not to depend on a man—I did that, but no one told me how to be a wife. No one told me how to love a man or how to choose one. No one explained to me what was important in a man or how I should be with this man once he married me and my success. No one!

I was told to wait on Jesus. I was told that Jesus would make my decisions and even bring a man to me. Never once did anyway make me responsible for my decisions on who I brought into my life... So, wait on Jesus I did, and nothing happened for a long time.

I have so many friends who I counsel daily with issues in their relationships and when we are honest and look at our lives, we realize we all came from dysfunction in the highest degree, so who would have told us? I am telling you that once you stop acting like you know what you are doing and start being honest about what you want and don't want, you will never ever meet and marry the man that God has created you for. So, now that we have gotten that out of the way, let's do this, shall we?

I have done my own analysis and have come to some conclusions. Nine out of ten women will lie to themselves and to anyone who asks about their singleness, especially if they are attractive, successful and well educated. You lie. Admit it. Okay, I already can see that you need help remembering the lies, so let me help you remember some of the things you say or have said:

"I don't need a man; I can take care of myself!!" Meanwhile you attract the most unprepared to be a husband, no job, no ambition guys out there. They seem to flock to you like bees to honey!

"I'm waiting on Jesus!" Meanwhile, you will hang out in a club with your girlfriends knowing that if Jesus had somebody, he would not be at the club!

"I can take care of my kids myself; I don't want a man in and out of their lives!" Meanwhile there are men in and out of your bed!

"We aren't serous like that! I don't care that he is seeing other women, I am too busy to be tied down anyway!" Yet you get upset when he doesn't call, can't remember your birthday and will never seem to find the time or have the attention span to give you any consideration!

"I am tired of these men out here! I can do bad all by myself!" If you are so tired, why do you cry begging God to send you somebody?

"He just needs some encouragement, and I believe I can help him!" Never mind the fact that he has no ambition, no job or career, no plan and no commitment to you!

What's so sad about successful Black women is they can be just a tragic as those on government assistance, and the only difference is a degree, a job and a luxury sedan. Successful Black women are having babies from random bootie calls just like women who are on SNAP. Successful Black women will overspend money and live beyond their means just like the welfare girl from around the way. Successful Black women are dealing with the same issues; being successful has not insulated them from the tragedy that replays generation upon generation in our community. Unless we conclude that we need to do things differently, like being honest, we will never be whole or happy.

Would it kill you to admit that you are ready for a meaningful relationship that has marriage as its destination? Can you admit to yourself or anyone else that you would very much like to be in a relationship where your husband is the breadwinner and you can focus on your home and your kids? Stop acting like your career is so fulfilling that you would rather work at the office with people who despise your very guts than to build an amazing family with an awesome husband. We wear our accomplishments like a of badge of honor that is supposed to entitle us to no worries but that is not realistic and, frankly, most good men are over it. How about saying to a man you just met, "I am only open to someone that could see himself being a father figure to my kids because their dad is not in their lives! I figured I would get that out of the way now to keep us from starting something that is going nowhere!"

It's as if the truth will betray you if you admit it. We have got to come to grips with the fact that when you lie to yourself, you give these men you are meeting permission to lie to you as well, whether he knows you are lying or not. You put that reality in motion because you are lying and the chances are you will be lied to.

At some point, we have to be ready to stop these types of relationships before they start because they are built on shaky ground from day one. Our encounters are so few and far between that we don't want to ruin an opportunity to have somebody—anybody in our lives, no matter how short lived the time he is there. These types of encounters will always keep you occupied to the point that if you were to meet someone who had quality, you would miss them because you are all caught up in Mr. Wrong!

Don't get it twisted! Just because you are educated and in a great career, doesn't mean that the guys that you will be exposed to are any more mature or ready to settle down as the guy spending all his money on his car and his clothes while living at home with his mama. We should recognize that there is a problem with our understanding of our roles in relationships and the methodology persists no matter where you are on the economic spectrum. Once you get into the habit of telling the truth about what you want and how you want to live, there will be a wonderful transformation in your life.

Place Values, Part 2

It's through the lies that we get caught into the cycle of ending up where we never really intended to go. This leads to saying and taking on beliefs that we really don't mean to adopt as facts in our lives. The cycle will continue if we are not careful to just call the thing—THING!

This is where what we value once again comes into play. It's no secret that we lie to ourselves because it's so apparent in our behavior. Recently, Steve Harvey had two young ladies on his talk show who dressed provocatively and then would take pictures of themselves and post them on Facebook. Both ladies were single, and both claimed they were looking for nice guys who could see the beauty that they had inside of them.

Steve, to help them see that the very nature of their behavior, would never yield what they professed that they wanted, tried to show them through the testimony of real men viewing the photos, showed the ladies that they were far from where they said they wanted to go.

The ladies watched and listened to these total strangers describe them as sluts and promiscuous... cute, pretty, and beautiful were some of the words that came from these men. When Steve asked them if they would ask them out, all said no. They all felt that these were not the kind girls you take home to meet Mama. You just have fun with them and leave it there.

There girls seemed unchanged in their thinking. They truly believed that the right man would see the photos and immediately want to get to know them and eventually marry.

I am sure, if pressed in a private setting, these girls would have admitted that the only attention they receive is from men who wanted to have fun with them and leave.

Once again, when you lie to yourself, you tend to do the very thing that pushes you away from what you say you want. It's through truth that we find true love.

Place Values, Part 3

We say we want so much, but we have to understand that our actions speak so loudly. Our actions literally undermine everything we say we want. We want good men, but we devalue them with our very actions as women. We have to raise the standard in order for men to hold each other accountable for the way women are treated in the entire community.

What's behind the devaluation of men? It's almost four hundred years in the making for Black women. Even the presence of Caucasian and Latino men in the family isn't valued as high in recent years. The social ramifications of missing men in the Black community has been well documented for decades, but the issues that come with missing men are reaching beyond the Black community. White and Latino families are feeling the pain as well.

The Department of Economic and Social Affairs, a division of Social Policy and Development for the United Nations put out a statement in 2011 that I found amazing and needs to be shared over and over:[16]

In Chapter 2 of the "Men in Families: A Family Policy in a Changing World," the authors consider the subject of fathers and father figures, and their changing roles in different cultural contexts, with attention being drawn to the concept of "social fatherhood," which encompasses the care and support of males for children who are not necessarily their biological offspring. The chapter reviews different forms of father engagement and their implications for children and families, including the evidence of the beneficial educational, social and psychological effects on children. It looks at men and fathers across generations while considering the consequences of the growing numbers of older persons for families, intergenerational relations and childcare. The chapter further explores what is known about work-family balance with respect to men, and the role of policy in advancing men's engagement with children in the context of employment policies. Men's mental and physical health is also considered and research pointing to the benefits to men arising from their engagement in family life and their relationships with their children is reviewed. The final section outlines the implications of these issues for social and family policy within the context of the labor market, law, education and health and social services. All social and family policies should contribute to creating an environment in which men, and women, have family time and the opportunity to care for and engage with their children, and the support needed to do so. Consistent with the Convention on the Rights of the Child, laws and policies must ensure that children are protected and cared for by both parents, including under conditions of adoption, fostering, custody and maintenance. It is especially important that labor laws and housing and financial regulations facilitate men's involvement with and support for their children and families. In addition, government, the private sector and civil society must enable and encourage men to take advantage of legal, labor and other provisions that support men's participation in childcare and family life. Formal education and informal sources of influence, including the media, play a critical role in constructing and maintaining social norms and attitudes, including regarding the roles of fathers in the lives of children. Health services should recognize that men make many health-related decisions affecting their families and target them by nutrition, immunization and other health-promoting messages. Social services facilitating fathers' participation in childcare, early child development programs, school and after school programs should be advanced as well. Lastly, as significant changes occur in the domain of social and family policy, it is essential that they facilitate men's contribution to children's health and development and family well-being—but only in ways that do not unwittingly lead to a further entrenchment of men's tradition-based control over women and children.[16]

Imagine that! The United Nations sees the value of a man in the home, but you don't?

We have to acknowledge that there are so many factors that have kept our families—men, women and children—all broken, but it's through thought and truth telling that we can change it all, one encounter at a time.

We have to decide that we will stop perpetuating the problems by acting contrary to what we say we want. If you don't want to be a crackhead, you definitely would not hang out in a crackhouse all night long. Growing up, my grandfather use to say, "If you ain't selling nothing, take ya' sign down!"

We have to do a better job of being honest about what we say we want.

I cannot tell you how much I owe to the solemn word of my good mother.
-Charles Spurgeon

5

Single Mama Drama

I started entertaining the insanely stupid idea of having a child alone. I'm talking about looking for a guy to just have a baby with, no strings attached – just because I wanted to have a baby. Now, it's one thing to make a mistake and get pregnant and then live with the consequences of those actions, but it's an entirely different thing to decide to bring a baby into your world planning not to have a father there as well.

I thought about guys that would be great sperm donors. I thought about how it would feel to pick up my son or daughter from preschool in my Lexus IS. These images started flooding my brain. Then it happened.

I was invited to a baby shower by a friend having a baby with her boyfriend. She was college educated and even though she hadn't started her career just yet, she felt that motherhood would be a breeze.

While sitting at my table, I noticed a lady who had a little girl with her. (The Devil was setting me up with friends who were already on the road that I was entertaining! Beware of who suddenly becomes a part of your circle, but I digress!) We began playing baby shower games and discovered that we had the exact same birthday—month, day and year! We immediately started talking. She was a professional, just like me. She had graduated from college—just as I had and even gone to graduate school. After talking for a while, we came to the subject of her little girl. Her daughter was about four years old, but she had the mouth of a fourteen-year-old! She was a busy little girl, and she was constantly chiming into our adult conversation.

Before long, the mom had to pick the girl up and take her out because she was causing such a scene at the shower. When she returned, she said to me, "I have got to call her father because this girl is out of control!"

"Where is he?" I asked.

"Oh, he's around," she replied with a rolling of her eyes.

"So you guys are not together anymore," I inquired.

"No, we were really never together," she said, "I had the bright idea of having a baby by myself... biggest mistake of my life!" she said.

She seemed genuinely sad about her decision to have a baby on her own. After talking with her a bit more, she said that she made it clear when she decided to have her baby that her child's father wasn't required to do anything. She felt she had the money, she owned her own home, and she had her "dad" and her "brothers" to give her child the "male" influence that all kids need.

None of her plans were working. As a baby, her daughter was fine, but now that she could talk, there were problems. And that's what happens with most women who make that decision; they forget that these babies grow! It seems like one day you are mixing formula and the next, you are trying to decide on public or private school.

Most women totally play down the value of a man in a child's life. Why do we do that? Because society does it. We totally discount a man and the contribution of his presence in our families which is the saddest, most destructive view of our society.

We must be careful as successful Black women not to fall into the trap of valuing money, assets and access over a male's presence in the life of our children and more importantly—OUR LIVES.

We should be careful about our view of men because if you think you can make it without a man, you will be without one; whether you enjoy that lonely journey is totally up to you.

Remember, we have a long history in this country for being forced to live without men. The reality of this history has had negative consequences on both Black men, women, and children. We have to know that all have been effected by this crisis, but the storyline that is broadcast in the media that these issues are inherently a

Black problem is starting to unravel. Why? Because fatherlessness is not exclusive to the Black Community. The Huffington Post published an article in 2014 that really brought light to the myths that we constantly repeat as facts. In the article entitled, "5 Lies We Should Stop Telling About Black Fatherhood," Danielle Cadet made some interesting assertions that bare repeating.[17]

First, the lie that Black Fathers are not involved in their children's lives. This is just not true. Recent data published by the Center for Disease Control revealed that African-American fathers spend more time in their childrens' day-to-day lives than dads from other racial groups, defying stereotypes about Black fatherhood. The Pew Research Center has found similar evidence that Black dads don't differ from white dads in any significant way and that there isn't the expected disparity found in so many other reports. Although Black fathers are more likely to live in separate households, Pew estimates that sixty-seven percent of Black dads who don't live with their kids see them at least once a month, compared to fifty-nine percent of white dads and just thirty-two percent of Hispanic dads.

The second lie is that single parent homes are a Black problem that's epidemic! Not true!

The increase in the number of single-parent homes has repeatedly been painted as a problem exclusively rooted in the Black community. However, that fact couldn't be further from the truth. The number of single-parent American households has tripled in number since 1960, and while an overwhelming majority of these households are likely to be led by Black or Hispanic women, the number of Black, single-father households is also on the rise.

The next lie points to the morality of the Black female and her willingness to be a mother without a husband. The article points out that:

According to a 2010 study, seventy-two percent of Black children are born to unwed mothers, a sharp contrast to the twenty-four percent detailed in the 1965 Moynihan Report.

Some have taken this number and cited it as a contributing factor to a large portion of Black America's present-day plight. However, many have taken issue with how this statistic has been used with respect to the Black community's moral standing. In an article for The Atlantic, Ta-Nehisi Coates broke down the numbers to give a more accurate depiction...

"But while the number of unmarried Black women has substantially grown, the actual birthrate (measured by births per thousand) for Black women is at the lowest point that it's ever documented.

While a larger number of Black women are choosing not to marry, many of those women are also choosing not to bring kids into the world. But there is something else.

As you can see the drop in the birthrate for unmarried Black women is mirrored by an even steeper drop among married Black women. Indeed, whereas at one point married Black women were having more kids than married white women, they are now having less.

I point this out to show that the idea that, somehow, the Black community has fallen into a morass of cultural pathology is convenient nostalgia. There is nothing "immoral" or "pathological" about deciding not to marry.

To me, the whole point of this book drives at the heart of the last part of the quote above from Coates. Even the most prepared of us as women—those who are married and educated and have the means to decide to do something different with our kids that would change the negative narrative about the Black family chose NOT to have kids because of all the bad that has happened in the past of so many women from wounded communities.

I am not advocating marrying just anybody, I am championing the idea that our decisions need to be rooted in the preservation of who we are. I look at the children who need help understanding why our culture is so worth preserving. It amazes me how our culture is so coveted by so many outside of our community yet we are willing to augment it through our selfishness and lack of love for one another.

Coates further points out, "The effect fatherlessness has on children's lives. Children in father-absent homes are almost four times more likely to be poor, and being raised without a father raises the risk of teen pregnancy, marrying with less than a high school degree, and forming a marriage where both partners have less than a high school degree. However, men who didn't grow up with their fathers are not incapable of being good fathers themselves—an assumption disproportionately assigned to Black men who are more likely to be raised by single mothers."[18]

The Redirect

It is high time that Black women get a reality check. There are Black men out there, you just aren't feeling any of them because your focus is on what we have come to believe as fact! Not who they are and what they can become with the right woman! If we were honest with ourselves, we would know and understand that there is a conspiracy going on. Sure, Black women are more successful than Black men! Our society doesn't value a brother and never has. And we—as women—add insult to the injured Black men by putting expectations on them that are unrealistic in addition to our complete need to be in full control of every situation.

Let's face it, we don't trust our men to be husbands or fathers. We don't trust them to take care of business; therefore, we don't expect them to. And because we don't expect them to—they don't! It's easier to believe that he will become what our society says he will become. Our families will die a quick death if we, as African American women, don't change our view! Sure, we aren't all the blame, but we can help shift the paradigm by not perpetuating negative and incorrect information. We must do it now or we will never realize our dream of a marriage or family that we desire for ourselves.

*If you don't understand
yourself, you don't understand
anybody else.*
-Nikki Giovanni

6

What is a Wife?

_____

A wife is required to be many things. Strong, but soft and vulnerable. Vocal—yet slow to give every thought she is thinking. Creative, frugal—yet lavishly intuitive. Wives work, but they make time to be lovers and mommies. Wives share without even a thought of themselves or their needs. A happy wife can move an entire community to step in tune to her will. Wives have power that women only dream of. Why? Because wives have a Divine Ordination that comes from the very position that she has been placed in.

In Proverbs 31:10 it says: How hard it is to find a capable wife! She is worth far more than jewels! Her husband puts his confidence in her, and he will never be poor.

What is so interesting to me about this passage is that it clearly states that finding a good wife is hard—not finding a good husband. It appears when we read the entire chapter in Proverbs, that a wife truly makes the husband. Verse 11 says, because of the wife, "he will never be poor."

I point out these points in scripture because we have been focused on the wrong things when it comes to marriage and family in the context of Proverbs 31.

First, we have had horrible examples and the wrong definition of being a wife continually propelled into mainstream culture. You may think you want to become wife, but if you do a little research, you may discover that you are woefully unprepared.

In Genesis 2:18, it states *The Lord God said, "IT IS NOT GOOD FOR THE MAN TO BE ALONE. I WILL MAKE A HELPER WHO IS JUST RIGHT FOR HIM." ANOTHER TRANSLATIONS READS: "IT IS NOT GOOD FOR THE MAN TO BE ALONE. I WILL MAKE A HELPER AS HIS COMPLEMENT."*

A compliment to a man... not a mother, not a partner, not a boss, not someone who can change him, compete with him or complete him—but a helper, to suit HIS needs. Many women have the wrong idea about being a wife and what the Bible is describing. We often dismiss the Word of God as old and out of touch, but for those of us who are married and get it, we see that this description is amazingly on target.

We may assume that our goals, our ideals, our ambitions should come before those of our husbands—or that they are equally important. I submit to you, that when you are happily married, it doesn't take long to understand that God has a plan for your family, and everything must work together till that end. I know what you are thinking! You think I have fallen back in the Stone Age and I am crazy! But hear me out.

The year was 1999. I had finally met a man who was not intimidated by me. He was handsome and intelligent. He was college educated and well-traveled. The only problem I could see was that I clearly made more money than he did.

Oh, the gap was wide, ya'll... like an ocean—wide!

I was so arrogant too... I didn't have the patience to wait on him to get it together, either. I wanted him to have it together with the quickness because I had plans that did not include waiting. He needed to already own a home, and it needed to be bigger than mine. He needed to have a nice car—and it needed to be nicer than mine—all the things that would have just made our relationship perfect and easy. To me, and to most women, that was being a wife. Finding someone who will allow me and what I brought to the table to fit together in a neat little package that looked great.

Here I was, a six-figure income earner, multiple home and car owner and he was living with his cousin working hourly at a telecommunications company. Living in Miami didn't help, either. Whenever we went out, I had to find ways that we could go to dinner or a movie without making him feel like a failure. How could we go to South Beach or Coconut Grove to the kinds of restaurants that I frequented without making him feel as though he was way out of his league? Well, I made a decision that most sisters would say is totally out of the question. I decided, we just won't go out.

I started to save my money, and I decided not to focus on our financial differences. I cooked more. Every night I came home from work, I cooked dinner at my house and he went home to his apartment with my leftovers. Not only did I improve my cooking skills, our time spent together wasn't a daily reminder that I made more money. Instead, I helped inspire him every day to strive for his own personal improvement.

You see, we place so much value on money and so little on the relationship and how it can be used to further—not only the Kingdom of God, but the community that we live in. Our misguided focus makes our relationships fragile and difficult to survive without money. If we value money more than relationships, we won't have much of anything if the money goes away. Value your man, and he will become more valuable than anything you or he could ever have. If you plan to be with him forever, you have to build a forever relationship... and trust me, you won't always have money.

In our society, we have so many messages about relationships that are selfish and unsupported by loving principles—let alone the Bible. Before I learned what a wife truly is, I felt being a wife was having a man who could handle a "strong Black woman." Like he needed to be stronger than me; ladies, marriage is no competition! I used to believe that he would have that great career and he would have great credit so that we could buy anything we wanted. We would travel whenever we wanted and our kids would be in private school. We both would have careers, so whenever necessary, I would bring in a nanny to watch the kids whenever our schedules didn't give us that extra time. Oh, and our kids would be perfect.

We would be stern, but loving—all while raising these globally conscience little, bilingual angels who never misbehaved. I would show the world how easy it is to have a great career, a fabulously fine husband that made more money than I did. We would be the power couple with the great home in the suburbs. That was my vision of being a wife and I am sure if you picked up this book because of the title, it is probably your vision too—or a vision that's pretty close! I am here to tell you that you are so far in left field that even the bleachers are nowhere in view!

Your Purpose in Marriage

"And we know that all things work together for good to them that love God, to them who are the called according to his purpose." (Romans 8:28).

It is hard for me to imagine anyone not wanting to know their purpose here on this earth. How could anyone feel good about aimlessly existing in a world that's cold and uncaring about any and every thing. People are dying daily—people who are good, honest, loving... mothers, fathers, brothers, professors, children—no one seems exempt. Even I have tasted death. I tremble as I say that because at first, I refused to admit it—even to myself... but I have, and so here is my testimony.

Here is what I know... there are gifts that God gives to all of us. Then—there is purpose. Many sing, but that doesn't mean that you are called to record an album. Many write, but who's to say that you are to be an author. Gifts are often translated—wrongly into purpose.

Now, marriage makes it even trickier. You see, I am a bit old fashion in my thinking. As a married women, it took me much prayer and humility to realize that as a wife, I have been instructed to help my husband. Now, before you ladies give me the side eye—here me out. I believe that we will find our purpose in making ourselves available to help our husbands with the mission that God has placed on *his* heart. Marriage is a ministry in and of itself. If we are listening attentively to the Spirit of God, we would hear His call and leading as couples to a task that He has ordained... I'm still talking about purpose—so stay with me.

After almost nine years of marriage, I realized what I was supposed to be doing to help my husband. I know because the enemy himself came against us...

My husband works in finance. He has always worked in finance. He has a degree in finance and he lives and breathes the stuff. I have never been big on numbers, so I have always stayed out of that lane. My thing was and still is advertising and marketing. For almost twenty years, that is what I did and still do between home-school and developing recipes.

Last August, my husband took our boys and me on a working vacation to Bermuda. What's funny is, up until that point, I never had a good explanation for what my husband did because I never really saw him do it. I knew he helped people save money, and I knew he helped people make money, but because I was a new mom, I was never in the room to hear or see what he did. I was always chasing one of my boys. This time, God decided to show me what my husband did and how I could help him do it—better—and to the Glory of God.

My husband's cousin, who lived in Bermuda, offered to keep our kids so that I could go with Jason—alone—to dinner. My husband, who is a workaholic, took me to dinner all right—he just neglected to share that we needed to stop by—not one, but two clients on the way. I didn't get upset, I just went, and for the first time I got to see him in action—uninterrupted, no distractions. It was as if my eyes were opened. Light bulbs were literally going off in my head. My excitement and sheer awe of what he did have me brain flashing one hundred miles per minute! Over dinner and all the way home, my mind and my mouth were churning out idea after idea as to how the church needed to hear his concepts and his strategies on making and saving money. I imagined what life would be if the church wasn't always raising money. What if we taught the Body of Christ how money worked—in the world—and how we can leverage those concepts to help the people of God do His work.

"But the Church has heard it," my husband kept repeating. "No, Jason, we need to say it in a different way," I told him. And I went to work. Long story short, by January 2015, I had rolled out a new website, new logo and new slogan. We had a new company name and a new marketing strategy. Using some of my old marketing contacts, I had churches, real estate and mortgage companies lined up—all to realign our focus and unveil my husband's new vision for teaching families how to make their money smarter.

Future Family Finance was born. Our slogan, "Passing Wealth to the Next Generation," became our mantra. I was so excited, we bundled the boys up in the car and hit the road. I would sing, he would speak and share his financial concepts—and we were doing it well. Churches and individuals were learning how they could cut their interests cost on all their interest baring loans. We were telling the people about Ellen White and sharing quotes from Counsels on Stewardship to Adventists and Non Adventist—we were on fire. We were surpassing our client acquisition from 2014 by wide margins, and the company was healthy and breaking all sales goals.

It was mid-June, and we were headed to Orlando for a three-week series and while on the way my husband shared with me that he hadn't come up with a sermon title for the church we were going to.

"Okay... " I said. We were about five days out, and he had nothing. He was supposed to speak at 11 a.m. the following Saturday and then that afternoon he was to do a seminar. I was going to sing and just help him manage it all. He said to me, "What do you think about you doing it and I just do the seminar in the afternoon. "Doing what?" I said. "Preaching?" (I am still talking about Purpose.)

On my tongue was an emphatic, "NO!" but in my heart, I was open... so I said, "Hmm. Let me pray on that."

Sure enough, God gave be something that I needed to study. I wrote the sermon, "Desperate Housewives of Canaan," and so it began. For the next three weeks, I was preaching and people were giving their hearts to Christ. The spiritual high was amazing and humbling. I was constantly checking myself. I wanted to hear God tell me what to do next. As we got closer to the end of the three weeks, I realize that what I was saying was not coming from me. I was reminding the people that there is a time of trouble coming... money will be thrown in the streets... there will come a day when we will not buy or sell without the mark. I was telling people you must be mindful of the loans that you are entering into. You are living as if you plan to stay here. Please, you must seek God and His counsel in these uncertain days...

We were gone for almost a month, and all of us were tired. The boys had had enough of Minnie, Mickey, and Goofy... They weren't even impressed with the hotel anymore. We were done with Orlando, and we all wanted to go home. As I study the calendar, I realized that I was getting dangerously close to my deadline. You see, I had made plans to go to the General Conference of Seventh Day Adventist session in San Antonio, Texas. There were only a few days until the first Sabbath of General Conference and I needed to get home because I needed to get to San Antonio by that Monday. We had planned to leave Orlando the Sunday before, but Jason kept getting requests for meetings so we said we would leave Monday. Then I thought, well maybe I will fly out of Orlando to San Antonio. With this plan, I considered taking my one year old with me to make it easier on Jason. That night the Spirit of the Lord came over me, and I had a strong urging not to even bother with San Antonio.

"But, Lord, I argued, I have to go. My new cookbook was being featured in Message Magazine, I have a booth, I need to go..." Still, I felt even more strongly, "DON'T GO!"

I told Jason. He kept asking me, "Are you sure?" I assured him that it would be fine not to go. I felt it was what I needed to do. We just needed to get back home to Alabama from Orlando and we planned to leave Monday night, but still, more people were wanting us to stay. Finally, on Tuesday, I told my husband—we are checking out of this hotel and we will not be staying another night in Orlando. Today we must go home. All that day, more and more calls came for Jason to meet with people. Three o'clock came. Then six o'clock came. We were still in Orlando, and I could see he was going to be too tired to drive. Now, I had been married nine years at this time and I could actually count on one hand the hours that I had driven anywhere long distance with him. So, that lets you know that I had a problem if I was determined to leave that night.

I looked at Jason and said, "I'll drive." He was surprised but okay with the offer, and we prepared the boys to leave.

I went to McDonald's—I hate to say this—bought a medium latte and at 11:30 on Tuesday night, I entered the ramp of I-75 northbound. Everyone in the car was sleeping. I sang, prayed, talked to God, came up with more sermon ideas—all while driving. When I couldn't go anymore, it was 4 a.m. and I was in Adairsville, GA—north of Atlanta. Jason woke up and told me he could make it from there.

When I got into the passenger's seat, I had the headache of the century. My head was literally splitting, but I felt it was the coffee and I had driven all night. I tried to sleep, but I couldn't. The sun was rising and already we were getting calls to come back to Florida on our cell phones. By the time we got to Huntsville, I just couldn't take the headache anymore. I just knew that sleep was all I needed. When I got home, I unpacked, swept my front porch, organized the laundry, took a shower and planned to sleep until the next day (bear with me, I am still talking about purpose).

I laid down around 11:30 a.m. I didn't take anything for my headache. A friend and I had been texting, and she needed to know when I would be home to pick up something from me. I told her I was real tired, but to come on over and if I didn't answer the door right away, keep knocking because we were all inside sleeping. Around 12:45, sure enough, I heard her at the door. By now, my head was on another level of pain. I still felt like sleep was all I needed. She came into my house, and I remember her commenting that I looked funny and I seemed to be a bit disoriented. I explained to her that I had literally been up all night, how tired I was and that sleep would take care of it.

After she left, I again tried to sleep—but nothing—no position, no amount of pillows were comfortable to me. I was miserably tired. Later that afternoon, my in-laws invited us over for dinner, so we went. While talking to everyone, I complained that the room was so bright and that my eyes seemed to burn. It was more comfortable for me to talk with my eyes closed or covered—but again, I thought I was just tired.

When we got home, I was determined to get sleep, so I took an herb called Valerian Root. It's an herb that relaxes you. After a few hours, nothing, so I broke down and took two Advil. The pain let up a little, and I was at least able to fall asleep but by 1 a.m., I was in my bathroom throwing up. I remember walking to the bathroom in the dark. I threw up on the floor, and I could hear Jason say "ewww, that's not good."

Covered in vomit, I sat on the floor by the toilet. My heart began to cry out to God—I felt awful. I could hear Jason cleaning up the mess, and I remember thinking to myself, "Why won't he turn on the lights so he can see?" but I didn't think much about it because the pain wouldn't allow my focus to go anywhere else.

Jason cleaned me up, changed my clothes and put me back in bed. I tried my best to sleep, but I got nothing. The next day I didn't get out of bed. My headache had literally paralyzed me. My kids played in my bed around me. I didn't eat or drink anything... I just lay there, hurting. Later that day, my mother-in-law came by and insisted that I go to the hospital. So, when Jason came to my bedside to help me get dressed, he asked, "What do you want to wear?" I said, "Oh, there are some dresses in the closet to the left." He came to me and said, "What about this one?"

"Turn on the light for me," I said....

"What do you mean, it's four in the afternoon," he said.

"Well turn on the lamp," I said.

"What do you mean, Carmen—can't you see this?"

In a very dramatic moment of shock, I reached out into my personal darkness to touch my husband, and he was right in front of me. I gasped because the darkness that I saw was so complete and so unending. There were no shadows or silhouettes. There was no light and no edges. We quickly surmised that I was blind, but we didn't panic. Jason dressed me, and we headed toward the truck in the garage.

I felt as though, while walking through my living room, that I could see my furniture, light and everything. That just shows how funny the mind is. When I got outside, I could smell the summer heat and I felt the warmth of the afternoon sun, but I saw nothing. It was in that moment that I knew something was seriously wrong. Complete darkness is scary, especially when you consider that, unless you have been blind, you have never seen before. No shadows, no streaks of light or color... nothing.

When we arrived at the doctor's office (I went to my primary care physician first—stubborn, I know), it wasn't long before my doctor came in and examined me. With the most tender touch and a voice that was stern yet caring, my doctor advised be to go immediately to the Emergency Room not far away. I remember the care in his voice... and the touch. It felt as though he was touching me for the last time.

Jason quickly got me back to the car, and we headed to the hospital. While there, the doctors seem stumped at what could be causing the blindness. I could hear them rushing around in an urgent panic. Test after test and soon sincere concern came in the voice of the physician. Something is not only wrong, but very wrong.

"We can't help her here," the doctor said. "We don't handle enough cases like this." "She needs to go the Nashville."

"Why Nashville? Why so far away?" my husband inquired.

"Well, that's where we send patients that we can't handle," the doctor explained.

"Can you at let least check UAB in Birmingham?" my husband asked.

"I will check," the doctor said.

Sure enough, after calling both hospitals, Vanderbilt in Nashville had a two day wait, but UAB in Birmingham could take me immediately.

So off to Birmingham I went—in an ambulance. I can't even explain the craziness of that ride. I had been to Birmingham many times, so at every turn, I tried to imagine where we were. In my darkness, I could hear the driver and the conversations he was having with the guy inside the back with me. We were riding very fast, and I could hear the sirens. There are mountains and steep hills between Huntsville and Birmingham, but never did they feel so big to me. In my darkness, they seemed enormous. After the craziest ride of my life, I finally arrived and I was immediately prepared for surgery.

Doctors everywhere were asking me, "Can you see this—Can you see that?" There was a little improvement but nothing more than shadows.

Finally, I could hear my husband's voice. So calm and so steady. Jason has always had a way with me, and he helped me to not panic. Doctors and nurses were everywhere. They had figured out what was wrong with me and the plans had been made what to do. I had a pituitary tumor that had begun to hemorrhage. Before long, they were asking me to relax and I felt myself falling off to sleep.

When I woke up, the light was so incredible, it felt blinding—but in a good way. I could see, and my husband and his mom were right there. The light was just a welcomed sight that let me know that the worst was behind me. My ordeal was amazing and even now while I write this was an incredible challenge with all kinds of emotional ups and downs.

After several days, I was finally allowed to go home but not without questioning God and why this all happened.

I maybe learning new things daily about my life, my purpose and my marriage as I continue to grow, but I can tell you what I know right now: there is a steady beauty that comes with being married to someone who not only loves you but genuinely has your best interests at heart. Someone who wants you and will challenge people who don't know you to do more than their best to care for you.

I have been told that if I had gone to Vanderbilt, my vision would have likely been permanently affected. Now, that's serious. I asked my husband what made him question the doctors when they were thinking of sending me there... and he said, "I know that hospitals will do what's best for them first without always considering what's in the best interest of the patient." In other words, it's not that they wouldn't care for me, of course they would have provided care, but, if there is an underlying benefit for me to receive that care at one hospital rather than another, they would've sent me said hospital—even if it was not in my best interest.

Still, for months I questioned why. Why did all of this happen to me? The entire ordeal was life threatening. I could have died and any doctor would have told you that living would have been a miracle. Well, here is where being married to a good man that loves and appreciates you comes in...

In 2013, I developed a hernia. It wasn't terribly serious, so I scheduled outpatient surgery and had the hernia repaired. In 2014, I realized that, although I was slim, my stomach would not go down. Everyone assumed that I was pregnant again. When going back to my doctor, we discovered that the hernia was back and it was four times the size it was before. I was very discouraged, and I had no intention of going back into surgery. My doctor made me aware that I could live with this hernia, but it would be very uncomfortable over time and eventually I would have to get it dealt with.

My youngest son was a one-year-old, and I just couldn't imagine going back into surgery. Over time, I didn't feel pretty at all. My large midsection turned supersized in no time. I was so slim everywhere else and I know my husband was uncomfortable about it, but he never made me feel bad. It was in 2015 that I revamped my husband's company and changed everything. It was also in 2015 that I discovered the brain tumor.

Here is where the understanding of how God worked in our lives really comes to light... Jason was very understanding when it came to the dramatic change to my appearance. So many times, it crossed my mind to just go get a tummy tuck or something to help get me back to what I use to be. Jason didn't encourage that at all, and besides, I had already had a family member to do that and she died just days after the procedure. Despite it all, Jason encouraged me and he made me feel beautiful.

While in the hospital after my brain surgery, the cell phone rang—it was the surgeon who wanted me to do the hernia repair, which was a much bigger operation than the hernia surgery. Now, the simple hernia repair required a full abdominal wall reconstruction. I explained to the doctor that I was, at that moment—in the hospital and there was absolutely no way I could even agree to go back at that time. So, his office stopped calling. Months later, I asked my pastor, "Why? I wish I knew why this happened to me?" My pastor looked at me and said, "Sis. Carmen, He will reveal it in due time."

More months went by. Jason continued speaking and doing seminars, but because I was still recovering, he went without me. I couldn't believe I had put so much into revamping his company, and now I am out. I prayed one time, "Lord, why? Why did this happen the way that it did?"

In 2016, I discovered the pain from the hernia had gotten unbearable. I couldn't sit or lie down. Standing up was very hard to do after long periods of time. I was in pain, constantly. Jason would rub my feet and pamper me. He was an amazing support.

I finally scheduled in the surgery in May of 2016—over two years after the original hernia repair. The surgery was successful and both my sisters came to help me. It was a very serious surgery—more serious than the brain surgery. It took me weeks to just get out of bed on my own. There was the constant threat of blood clots so I had to get up and move around. After about three weeks at home, I had to go into the doctor's office for him to examine my bandages and the incision area to insure there was no infection. The doctor who did the surgery was out on vacation and another doctor came in that I remember seeing once in the hospital. He reviewed my chart asked a few questions and noticed there were notes in the file about the brain surgery.

He seemed curious about the surgery and began to ask me a few questions about it and then he said this:

"Well it sure is good that you got that brain tumor out of the way back in 2015 because if we had do this abdominal surgery before and your brain hemorrhaged while we were doing the surgery, it could have been fatal. Huntsville has no neurosurgeons that could have handled this, so it's a good thing you went to Birmingham to get this taken care of..."

Wait...what?

There was my why! Something that I would have never realized unless pointed out to me by a doctor. God allowed it all to happen the way that it did BECAUSE it could have been fatal any other way... and it's because God loves me so much that he put be in the best care possible! My neurosurgeon was the BEST in the southeastern United States! If I would have set an appointment, I probably couldn't have gotten him. He just happened to be on call.

How does any of this address your marriage?

When you are looking to get married, you will never know what lies ahead in your life. There will be ups and downs and there will be challenges—but your partner must be levelheaded and there to support you in ways that no one could ever prepare for. You just have to be in love. Love that is uplifting and reassuring. Love that is steadfast and inquisitive. Love that just doesn't accept challenges for what they seem to be, but will challenge obstacles prayerfully—knowing that everything isn't always what it seems.

Another thing to consider: there will always be lessons learned that will build character and help to shape your legacy in life. Also, situations will come to help you better understand yourself, your partner, your children and your God. What's interesting is, marriage is that one covenant that will help you better understand the mercy of God. What do I mean? Through the covenant of marriage your commitment opens you up to huge vulnerabilities, but those vulnerabilities show us just how God views love—in the most intimate of ways. God always likens the relationship of Christ and the Church to a marriage covenant. Christ is hurt by his bride but loved as well. There are ups and downs with this woman, but it's that love that keeps them together. The reason why I am trying to help successful Black women understand why it is necessary to rethink our view of marriage is just this point. We, as a community, have fallen out of love with the very relationship covenant, and we—as successful women—are the most prepared to be in the relationship. We have the resources to make the relationship more rewarding for all. We must not allow ourselves to get caught up in the crazy distractions that appear to be easier. Our community, our churches—all of us, everywhere need to do our best to change the conversation for the sake of future generations.

Don't just get married. Find a partner that you can dis-cover—together, your purpose.

Deal with yourself as an individual worthy of respect, and make everyone else deal with you the same way.
-Nikki Giovanni

7

That Guy You Never Called Back

Growing up in a small Floridian town was interesting. Good old Gainesville, FL. After college, I went back to Gainesville and soon I was working and living with my folks. Living in a college town, it wasn't long before I was dating again and the guy I was dating was in University studying to be a pediatrician. I found myself on campus at the University of Florida all the time, hanging out at the Student Union and it wasn't hard because I didn't look like a graduate.

My boyfriend, who shall remain nameless, had a friend named Brad who was interning at the hospital. Brad was a goofy guy who wore thick glasses and rarely dressed well. Every time I saw this guy he needed a haircut. He was nice but easily ignorable. He rarely commanded the attention of anyone, let alone a woman.

Even though my boyfriend at the time was in college, it wasn't hard for me to find friends who were just like me. I hung out with a group of girls who had all graduated and were working like I was. All of us were single and dating whenever we could. There was never a dull moment talking about the guys that we found ourselves dating. We were always complaining about the lack of men, and those we were meeting seemed to be in a perpetual state of "finding themselves."

Amongst those friends was a girl named Sherrie. Sherrie was gorgeous. She and I bought our first homes around the same time. She was the ultimate example of a woman who was doing it for herself. She had gone to college, rose quickly at a law firm where she worked and did everything from change the oil in her car to lay tile in her bathroom.

Sherrie and I hung out a lot, and we would always spend time at the Student Union on campus where my boyfriend and his goofy friend Brad would be.

Brad had been in college for at least ten years. He had wanted to be a doctor, but he kept having issues. Sometimes it was money, other times it would be family issues. It was always something keeping Brad from finishing school. In addition to his school woes, Brad couldn't buy a date. He was goofy, but underneath it all he was so nice; it just felt like he needed special attention to pull out the best in him. It wasn't hard to see the potential in Brad, I always figured he would eventually find someone because he was a really good guy.

I moved away from home after a few years, and Sherrie and I lost touch. I was working at a TV station in Tampa when I got the news that Sherrie and Brad were getting married. "WHAT?" I screamed while hearing my mother on the other end of my phone explaining what happened. "And you won't believe Brad, Carmen. He is so handsome. Sherrie really put him together. He wears the nicest clothes and has the most gorgeous smile. It's hard to imagine them without each other!"

While putting on my bridesmaid dress, I watched Sherrie get ready for her big day. All of us were helping her get dressed as she reflected on her time dating and getting to know Brad. She went on and on about how she could see his heart. She knew that he just needed support. She didn't try and change him or buy his clothes; she just inspired him and didn't make him feel like a failure. She went on to say she didn't focus on the huge differences in where they were in life. They just met at church and talked a lot and he got it together.

Now Brad is a hospital administrator for a group of hospitals in Northeast. They have two girls and are happier than ever. It's been over twenty years now and whenever all our old girlfriends get together, those who are still unmarried joke about how they wished they knew that Brad would have been so successful. If they knew, they would have at least called him back!

"Wow! These ladies still don't get it..." I say to myself as I listen to them go on and on about Brad.

Brad is successful because Sherrie believed in him. She wasn't with him because she thought maybe this guy will be successful someday. She was willing to love and support a man with potential—not promises. I saw that!! I saw you roll your eyes!

Listen, just because you sailed through school and got your great job doesn't mean you will meet a man that has done the same. Sure, they will be out there but isn't it time to stop excluding potential partners because you are tired of looking for potential? Our focus needs to be on things that are lost in many women's minds as important.

I can't tell you how important integrity is in any man! I just heard an Amen from Calcutta. I will take a broke man with integrity any day than a dishonest man with money! It's no fun wondering where your man is—especially when you know he has a propensity to cheat!

A man with a good work ethic goes a long way; I don't care if he cuts grass for a living! There is something that just cuts in your gut when you go to work and ol' dude is at the house—chillin'!

A man who honors you and celebrates you is a gem! Men who are insecure have a way of tearing you down and getting mad when you don't stay down!

What has happened to our radar when detecting the good and the bad in men? We celebrate the thug when we should tell the ol' boy to pull up his pants and close the door on the way out! We put up with infidelity as though it's necessary to have a piece of a man—because having no man is just not acceptable. We set the bar low because we assume that we lower our chances for meeting anyone and that is the furthest thing from the truth. We must retrain our thinking. Ask God to take the blinders off and open our hearts to His leading. We have to be willing to face that fact that our focus is skewed. We have very few relationships to look to as examples, and for those we have to look to, many are wounded and are just holding on. For those who are successful and have lasted the test of time, many of us aren't willing to do any of the things that they found necessary to make it.

Brad wasn't unique. He didn't get lucky, and Sherrie didn't win the lottery. Both were willing to do what many of us aren't willing to do... and that's be open. Being open doesn't mean sleeping around. Being open doesn't mean living together... being open means dating with standards and allowing God to speak to you about who he has created you for. Many of us drop the ball before we could ever get to that point in any relationship.

You see, Brad was working at a movie theater and dating an attorney. Many folks would have said there is no way that would have worked. Sherrie set her standards, and she lived her life. Brad rose to the occasion and got on track. For her patience and her standards, their relationship didn't derail his plans for getting himself together. Many women remove their standards as soon as they meet a potential man. Things get messed up because of premature behavior. Living together, having children and marrying too soon all will derail a good man, but Sherrie kept her head and was patient. Brad rewarded her with his love. Now, suddenly, Brad is fine! Brad looks good and is passing his classes. Brad is getting those promotions and doing his thing. Sherrie was successful in her own right, but she didn't compete with him. She complemented him and allowed him to lead her and their family even when her check was bigger than hers.

We have got to realize a man is only as much of the man his woman believes he is.

It's a tragedy how many good men are derailed due to premature behavior and a lack of standards. You, my sister, can change the narrative. You have the education, the resources, and the understanding that our future as a people depends on it. It starts with us because we carry way more power than we even know what to do with or how to leverage it.

Stop closing the possibilities of who you will marry or who you will date based on his car or the suit he wears. Those are trivial and silly reasons to close the door on a relationship. Then we get upset when that one guy you refused to even entertain blows up and is successful. Here you come looking desperate and needy, in classic "Gold Digger" fashion. We must do better! We are called to be better and we can be, starting right now.

No person has the right to rain on your dreams.
-Marian Wright Edelman

8

WANTED: A Healthy Black Family

_____

While pregnant with my second son, my husband and my eldest son loved to go swimming. We would go to the Health and Wellness center at a nearby University and swim on Sunday mornings. It would be so much fun.

One day, while swimming, a young Black female lifeguard was on duty watching us from poolside. We were the only people in the pool that Sunday, and I noticed that she looked at me—particularly—a lot. I figured she was concerned because I was seven months pregnant, but I soon learned that wasn't her reason for staring. I swam down to one end of the pool and my husband and son were at the other end near the lifeguard. It was at that moment that she took the opportunity to ask my husband a question. Soon my husband, who is a natural talker, was in full conversation with this young woman and it wasn't long before he was out of the pool, speaking to her while she seemed mesmerized, hanging on his every word.

Since no one said anything to me, I kept on swimming. Later, I asked my husband what she was so intrigued about. He said, "She asked me if we were a family."

"What?" I gasped.

"A family! She wanted to know if you were my wife and if these were MY kids." He further explained, "She said she had never ever seen a Black family in real life before."

"Are you kidding me?" I asked. "How old is she?"

"She said she is a senior at the University," he continued.

How on earth, in this day and age, could a twenty-two-year-old women, live life and NEVER, ever meet, know or see a Black man married to a Black woman with two Black kids that they both created together. How on earth is that possible?

It's possible because we as Black people have never completely understood our role is perpetuating the negative impact that has been forced on us—yes, by racism—yes, by poverty and lack of education and racism—yes, by systematic legislation that made it okay to have homes with no man in them... But also, by us! Yes, we begin to be okay with that narrative and we began normalizing destructive behaviors designed to destroy generations of family. We have had few examples and many of us are still affected by the mental scares of those who have lived before us. The role of a woman as a wife must be witnessed and emulated; it is a lifestyle that should be celebrated.

Even if we struggle to see these images, we are savvy and educated enough to know that if we want to see significant changes that will help build the community, we have to view life—for ourselves—differently. No longer can we allow other people to write our story for us. No longer can we let people who hate us tell us who we are and educate our children. We must end the madness and know that the reason that we are distracted with our careers and our semblance of power and worth is a mechanism to further divide and destroy the cultural strength that we naturally display.

One day (and please let that be today) you will realize that you can, as a woman, change the direction of our families in this country. And here is how:

1. Ask God to help you—because we all must upgrade our thinking about ourselves and about our people in general. Stop allowing reality shows to be the height of your own reality. Be mindful that what you consume, visually, physically and spiritually—becomes your reality. You should not desire dysfunction. Having a broken life with multiple twist and turns should not be what you attract for yourself.

2. If you want to marry and be happy and healthy, your agenda should be to help facilitate the plan the man that God connects you to. If he has no plan, then you must empower him to make one—not make one for him. Remember, men are broken to. In many cases, men have a complicated mix of distractions that are designed to keep them rethinking themselves and their goals. We can debate why that is, but

the point of this conversation is to help change the narrative for the female seeking to marry. This is hard for most women. If you are a strong, independent, career woman 'making it happen' down at the office, it's hard to not have all hands-on deck at the crib! When a brotha' aint making it happen, it's very difficult to step back because there is a delicate balance between helping him and stepping in and just doing it for him! You must not overstep your boundaries!

3. Understand that wives create the environment that inspires husbands to think, plan and strategize how he will lead your family closer to God and His plan for your lives. Nagging has been proven on so many levels not to work! So, you have to find a way to allow your man to find his way and he has to feel that you will follow where he leads.

4. Embrace his plan! Remember, God created men to lead, not be led. There is nothing more unattractive than a man who is married to his "mama." Don't be influenced by the images you see of Black men as 'hen pecked,' indecisive, weak, and unsure. Remember Brad and Sherrie? A good woman beside a good man is a powerful duo that has limitless potential. Don't be weary. Your power will be recognized soon enough, but let this man know that he has your unwavering support and when God blesses him, that blessing will fall all over you, I promise!

Once you take these initial steps, you will see that your husband will step up to the plate and deliver. Yes—your husband! The one you haven't met yet. He will need time, but he will realize the position that God has ordained him to be in. You must step back, relax, and let nature take its course.

Ever since I took this approach, I feel lighter. I feel more secure—not less secure—and completely comfortable with allowing our family to be led by my husband. Does he ask me my opinion? Of course, he does! Do we make joint decisions? Absolutely! Are there decisions that he leaves up to me? All the time! What happens to most women is they assume that this approach will leave them vulnerable to a misguided man who is selfish and unconcerned about his family. If that's your man, then you have the wrong man.

Across the African Diaspora, Our Cultures Collide

I observe women. Traveling and lecturing, doing seminars and coaching individuals has allowed me to be keenly aware of people, especially women. My own observation of people of color are in no way scientific, but I am sure will get you thinking a bit.

Women often struggle to adapt to cultural challenges because we craze security. Women are creatures of obedience—naturally. We are not big on taking chances with new concepts because we don't want to leave ourselves open for conflict or hurt. Who we are and what we believe is so etched into our cultural teachings that have been handed down—often by women who themselves struggled with the inability to adapt to changes. Now, to illustrate these changes, imagine with me women of color from around the world.

Let's examine for a moment how these woman wash dishes. Here me out on this...

Most women from the West Indians will run water in an open, unstopped sink and wash their dishes with a sponge and soap, rinsing after each dish is washed. Black women from the United States are more likely to run water in a stopped sink adding soap to the water and using a rag to wash dishes. Then, they will rinse the dishes in the adjacent sink filled with clean, clear water. Now African women are interesting. They will wet a sponge, add soap, and wash the dishes in a soapy lather and set them all aside—all soapy, then at once they rinse.

I know this because I have watched these different styles of washing dishes, and I have wondered why. What are the things that make these practices so universal no matter where these women of these three backgrounds are currently—compared to where they are from or how they were raised.

It hit me one day while taking a raft ride along a small unpopular river in Jamaica. We had just come from a small house where my husband's cousin took us to meet some family. There, a woman and some children were waiting in a house that was in the midst of construction. There were fruit trees and animals, like goats and a chicken or two. The house had a cistern, but the kitchen was under repair. A small rolling brook was nearby, and they didn't hesitate to use it. Everything from washing clothes to dishes was done in the free-flowing water, and it got me to thinking... "This is why West Indian women run the water while they wash the dishes." Water runs freely in the islands. When washing clothes or dishes, the water is running—clean and clear. Then when it comes to women in Africa, it makes since that they would soap up the dishes all at once and then rinse them at the end because water is not always easy to come by...

As an African American myself, there was always a basin at my grandmother's house filled with soapy water and a clear basin for rinsing. African American women got water from a well to wash clothes and dishes... a basin with soap and a clean and clear one for rinsing—hence, the reason why my observation made since to me, once I thought it through. Which leads to the question, we as women are taught how to wash dishes, in many ways, unknowingly, and although we all currently live in America why have those generational practices not changed? There are no shortages of water here (unless you are in California) yet, the African women wash the dishes the way they do because that is the way that makes sense to them. It isn't wrong. It will still get the dishes clean. In the same way, as an African American, most of us can relate to our elder women having a basin of soapy water that stayed in the sink all day long.

This is an example that may seem silly, but think about it: how then have these three different backgrounds created distinct practices that are passed from generation to generation? In the same way, the generational influence on relationships in these communities shape how we as women relate to men? Background must be explored when we think about how we relate to men and how we have been taught relationships work.

You can't deny it, we are all African, but how you relate to the African man is shaped—literally by where the boat dropped you off.

I get concerned about my African American men when I look at history and culture compared to African men or West Indian American men. Society writes off our African American men and often so do we. Is it all fair, though? In our previous example, we had to admit that we were all inadvertently taught how to wash dishes based on the environment. Resources changed, and we continued with what we knew.

In the same way, we must adapt to help save our culture and our relationships. We still are reacting to men and relationships as though we are victims of our environment, although men are educated and are seeking marriage. We still are acting as though single motherhood is expected, even though men want to be in committed relationships with the mothers of their children. It's not always fair to conclude that we are not responsible for our plight as unmarried women. We have to look at the conditions in which our people are currently and adapt to save the community.

If I didn't define myself for myself, I would be crunched into other people's fantasies for me and eaten alive.

-Audre Lorde

9

A Currency Called Intimacy

Ladies, can we talk? So many women have the amazingly wonderful power. While there are many who know of this power and abuse it, there are more who may be aware and then those who are clueless that I want to chat with. Let's have a candid conversation, shall we?

Growing up, we never used the "V" word. You know, the "vagina." I could never think of an appropriate time to use it. Anytime my mom or some other elder woman used it, I thought we were about to have some deep sexual conversation that I didn't want to have. Any time my friends used it, it felt like a dirty story was somewhere close behind. At school, I never liked to hear it because the snickering and laughter were just too uncomfortable for any serious conversation to be had. Then, there was the time while working at a radio station, I had the privilege of announcing on air that a woman name "Vagina Johnson" won our top prize.

Vagina! Vagina! Vagina! I've said it and you are reading it! There (but I digress...)

So, growing up, we changed the name of this female body part... hence, the Poonanie was born! (Pronounced "Poo' na – nee"). Okay, to be clear—Poonanie is truly a Black American slang, ebonics term that was born out of the very gut of the urban community. So, just work with me as I continue.

The Poonanie, for us, was like magic. It can make a boy notice you. It seemed to make even the plainest Jane the center of attention. There was real power in the Poonanie. Especially one that no man had seen, yet dreamed about. Men made up stories about an unseen Poonanie. They sat around and told tales as tall as the Redwoods about it. They envisioned what it looked like, how it smelled and even what it felt like. All men bowed to the unseen Poonanie.

But woe unto the woman who showed even a glimpse of her Poonanie. All power was gone. All the tall tales became hilarious whispers about the once allusive Poonanie. Men seemed to lose all interest in the Poonanie. All those who hadn't seen the Poonanie would often claimed they had after countless sighting by others.

It was always a sad day when a Poonanie lost its power. It was much like a fairy losing its wings or a star falling from heaven. Powerless Poonanies were defenseless against false claims of its sightings. Even when a Poonanie tried to defend itself, all its credibility diminished if there was even one shred of truth to anyone who claimed to have seen it.

Later in life, as I grew, I realized how powerful an unseen Poonanie truly was, especially as an adult. I saw how many women worked to get that power back while others felt they would use its implied power to get what they wanted out of life. Either way, there was a powerful lesson to be learned about the Poonanie. World wars were fought and lost because of the Poonanie, and once a woman learned it's power, whoa unto any man who desired it.

You can always tell a woman who understands the power of the Poonanie. There is a slight glimmer in her eye. She knows that there are men to be conquered if she could just hold on to her Poonanie. You have to be careful with any brother even catching a glimpse—even a glimpse can threaten its power.

Women soon learned how the Poonanie was in many ways like the most valuable currency on earth. I think you can now see where I am going with this...

You see a woman with a little money often attempts to control a man with that money in the same way she has learned to control with man with her sexuality. Money is power and so is the Poonanie. So, you may say, should I not protect my Poonanie?

Of course, you should! This conversation directs our attention to the danger that comes when we weaponized our wallets and our sexuality.

1 Corinthians 7:3-5 says, "The man should give his wife all that is her right as a married woman, and the wife should do the same for her husband: for a girl who marries no longer has full right to her own body, for her husband then has his rights to it, too; and in the

same way the husband no longer has full right to his own body, for it belongs also to his wife. So do not refuse these rights to each other. The only exception to this rule would be the agreement of both husband and wife to refrain from the rights of marriage for a limited time so that they can give themselves more completely to prayer. Afterward, they should come together again so that Satan won't be able to tempt them because of their lack of self-control."

It's no secret that women have discovered that there is some strategic benefit, either real or perceived to withholding sex from their husbands, boyfriends—men in general. It is in this context that a dangerous precedence begins for women who are trying to remain in control of men while in a relationship. This comes from a history of hurt. Remember, in our last chapter, we talked about how we are taught, whether we realized it or not, by cultural hang ups—even when the culture is transplanted to a new environment.

First, we as women must not be focus on relationship control in the first place. Men should be concerned about where the relationship is going, how the relationship is perceived and the very health of a relationship. (Ding Ding Ding—the bell that you hear ringing is the one in your head telling you that Leroy, Chase or Javier is NOT the slightest bit concerned about you, your relationship—where it is going or where it has been).

In the same way, women are now taking control of the romance and overseeing their own finance. Men are increasingly being held in the dark on their woman's financial status because of the control she struggles to release.

"This is MY money!" I hear it all the time when I am talking to women.

We must be very careful that we don't use the power of our money to control our relationships. Often, what you think is yours isn't and its perceived value is not that much. Many of us think that we have it all figured out with our separate accounts, our separate tax returns, and our prenuptial agreements, but how do you become one with someone that you don't even trust on your checking account? You will let him into your heart, all over your Poonanie but not into your 401K?

Does that make sense to you? Does it feel right to you? Are you so desperate that you would settle for anything similar to this? Let's start rethinking our power. Our power is best understood from a position of submission. By submitting, we better understand a man's need and his commission from God. By focusing on your place as a supporting cast member, you can truly see how your man's leading role will best be delivered. Use your power for good, the good of your family, the good of your community. When our focus is on ourselves, we lose an amazing opportunity to change the very direction of an entire generation of young people. There is no real power in your Poonanie or your Purse without love! Through the surrender of your heart to true love, you will realize that all God has blest you with just enhances your life with the man that he has created you for.

How Intimate is Intimate?

Jason and I talk about everything. Literally—everything. There is no subject off limits. We do everything together as well. When he goes on his business trips, he figures out a way that the whole family goes... that's just how much we love being around each other.

We love our kids. They are a challenge at time, but they love to be around us as much as we love to be around them.

Whenever we meet a couple that rarely spends time together, that is always odd to us. She is cool with him doing his thing and he is cool with her doing hers, that's just a red flag—especially when there is no desire to be close.

Remember, we are talking about a forever relationship. This is it! No one else. Till death do us part... forever!

How does a relationship that is okay with separation survive the forever?

I remember when I got sick. I had a brain tumor, and Jason was with me in the hospital talking with the doctors about my care. He was there with me every single day. Sleeping in a chair and eating that awful hospital food, but he was there with me. If I needed to go to the toilet, he was there... helping me get to the bathroom, bathing me and cleaning me. If I needed to use the toilet, he would help me sit on the stool, holding me and even wiping me afterward. The entire time I would think to myself "in sickness and in heath." We have both experienced taking care of each other in that way when we were down, that's the whole point of being on a team. When you are married, you are on a team and you are both in it to win.

On our team, I, my husband and my sons are all in it to win as a group. We know that the kids have the best shot at being successful if we stay together. I know that my husband will win at being a great father and leader of our team if I allow him to lead us. Jason knows that the best way for me to be a good wife is if he takes certain responsibilities from me. There are things that I don't worry about at all—like the mortgage or insurance payments or even savings.

When working together as a team, the quarterback isn't trying to be the center or the tight end as well. Everyone has a roll and when you love someone, in a relationship—especially when you want to win, you do what you can to ensure that they have what they need to do their part.

I said all that to say this: when you are dating and Ol' Dude is only interested in your rear end and not the whole you—there is a problem. When Mr. Wonderful only gives you information on a "need to know" basis of his movements or his whereabouts—that is a problem. When you catch a cold and you can't get him to at least run to the CVS on the corner to grab some cough medicine and sit with you until you feel a little better—you need to run, not walk away from Ol' Dude because life in a marriage gets hard. Whoever you marry should want to be there with you. They should want you to be happy. They should want you to be okay. They should never be okay with your pain or hurt. They must never be okay with your suffering or your loneliness. They must never be okay with you being unsure or unsafe. When you are in love with someone, you should be willing to do your part to show your partner that you are on their team and you want to win!

Even the Bible gives us a great way to understand roles and our positioning: "Just as each of us has one body with many members, and these members do not all have the same function, so in Christ we who are many form one body, and each member belongs to all the others. We have different gifts, according to the grace given us. If a man's gift is prophesying, let him use it in proportion to his faith." (Romans 12:4–6).

Or you can say: For now, you are all a family with many members. A husband, wife and kids do not have the same function, so in Christ, though many, we all form one family, and each of us belong to each other. We have different roles that we will bring to the family—according to how God has created us. If you are a husband, you lead and protect your family, if you are a wife, you support your husband and you are the first instructor for your kids.

I say this all because it never ceases to amaze me how both men and women miss the flags of a relationship that don't have what it takes to survive. I am shocked when I am speaking with a couple or even an individual and they make all kinds of excuses for why their oddities work and they will be okay. Only to come back to me later to say that they have grown apart.

God built men and women for relationship. We need to stop trying to build castles with Court Jesters with hopes that they would one day rise to be King!

You have to want a relationship. You have to want to win at it and whoever you decide to go into a relationship with has to want it to. You can't be trying to want it for him. There is no such thing as having *enough love for both you and him.*

Many of us are so concerned with the wrong things when we are looking for a mate. You are trying to make sure he has money and a career that looks good next to yours when you should be more concerned with if he wants to be next to you with or without that job! We get all caught up in his pedigree, and we lose sight of his eternal destination. Where are you going, and do you want to go with him and he with you?

Our focus is wrong! Stop watching *Being Mary Jane* and identifying *Gabrielle Union's* character! You must stop seeing yourself in the plight of the stereotypical unmarried successful Black woman. As of today, that is no longer who you are!

There are men who want to get married. They want to be in relationship just like you do. They are successful and searching. Why can't you find each other? It's because your criteria is flawed. You want a man with money and you just may find one who has money—but no integrity. Or he may have a great job, but he doesn't care for commitment. His resume shouldn't be your first inquiry. Integrity, a great work ethic, respect and self-motivation are all, hands down, more important than money any day. Which means, he shouldn't need to make a lot of money, if he is motivated to get up every day and work without being told! Honestly is sexy for a brother who may be starting up a small sales company, especially when customers write reviews about how great his work is and how well done it is.

Let me tell you about a couple that came into our offices looking for help. Meet Tammy and John. Tammy and John had dated briefly before. She was in law school and he was a want to be rapper and DJ. When she graduated and started working, he seemed to still be finding himself. She was always trying to get him to finish school. She was constantly trying to get him to match her and her accomplishments. Her moves made him feel as if she had no faith in him at all. After four years, he finally called it quits. She was so angry, and for years she was bitter—always going on about "guys who were going nowhere with these crazy "pipe dreams."

Well, John met Constance. Constance was young lady of Afro-Mexican heritage, she—culturally—saw John differently. After a year of dating, John and Constance got married and it wasn't long before he had finished school with a bachelor's degree, co-authored a book, and began public speaking.

Tammy saw him once on TV and couldn't believe it. "Why couldn't he get it together with me!" she yelled. Because Tammy, you were concerned about how he made YOU look, not how you made HIM feel!

Ladies, we must stop being concerned about where he is and catch the vision of where he is trying to go. Men need a good partner who will allow them to dream big. We are so concerned about what he can do—NOW and never want to be around for the journey of where he is going.

Marriage is just that, a journey, and when you are in it for the long haul, you are creative and inspiring—exactly what a man needs. Claire and Heathcliff weren't the Huxtables when they started out in marriage, they grew to be what we saw on TV. Most of us want to start out that way, but if you do, where do you grow to become?

When we started in marriage, my husband and I lived in a little two-bedroom condo. I washed clothes in a coin laundry and I worked in my husband's office answering the phones when he couldn't afford to pay anyone. Now, he has two business partners, an assistant and several agents working in his financial firm.

Marriage is a journey, but we are so concerned about seeing the end from the beginning that there are good men we are not allowing to date us—and many of them don't want to date you because you are more trouble than they want to take on.

Your focus is all wrong, and until you change it, you will never know what it means to be truly intimate with someone.

What women rightly long for is spiritual and moral initiative from a man, not spiritual and moral domination.
-John Piper

10

A Woman is Only a Woman When She Allows Her Man to be the Man

———

I was counseling a young woman who had been married for about ten years. She had met and married a close family friend that she had dated for several years long distance. She was a successful engineer, and he was a dentist. Both were Seventh Day Adventist Christians, and she had a daughter from a previous relationship. After being married for about two years they had a son.

Problems came quickly after their son's birth. He was a saver, and she was a spender. He was a stern disciplinarian, and she was a bit lax. It wasn't long before they both had different bank accounts and one account from which all their bills were paid. Her first rant in our discussion was, "If he would just put his half in the joint account when I tell him to, we wouldn't have any problems!"

"Wow," was all I could say. Then I explained to her that her statement alone was loaded with information that told me exactly what their issues were.

"You don't let him drive, do you?" I asked.

"Drive? What does that have to do with anything?" she questioned.

"You don't let the man drive when you go places together?" I asked again.

She then explained that they don't really go anywhere together. Even when they go to church, she drives in her car and he drives his. Once again, the signs were everywhere—this couple was on life support! At some point in our little talk I had to get her to understand that she was showing her husband distrust. She flat out did not trust him to do anything for her—from handling their finances to driving her to church. At first, she protested, but finally she had to admit it.

Now, I know this couple. I know him more than I know her, and I had to let her know that she was missing a huge blessing. You see, cultural differences play a role in this type of behavior. She is an African American, born and raised in the South—just like me. Culturally, women from the South are usually heads of the house or any many cases make many decisions about the family. Her husband was born and raised in Jamaica. Most Jamaican men are not likely to be led by a woman. Culturally, it's just not that common. This is where knowing your man comes in.

This may surprise you, but most men are basically the same. Your job is to know YOUR man. Pay attention because I need you to get this. All men are the same. Sure, they have individual charac-teristics—but all in all—it's the same dude, honey. So, before you trade him in for another, please know that the one that you think is better than the one you are getting rid of may end up being the same man. Hear me out:

Some guys pay attention to detail or are great at being handy—but for the most part they all hate to go shopping and they all want a plan of some sort that makes sense when going on a trip. Do you understand my point?

Think about it for a second. You have a friend who divorces her husband and then remarries a guy and has the same issues with him that she had with the first husband. That's because the issues she failed to work through in marriage number one will persist in marriage number two.

We must understand that marriage is a character building exercise that requires us to compromise, share, and learn to be patient plus a whole host of traits that can only come from being in a lifelong relationship. That's one of the main reasons why God made us the way he made us. We have to understand that, as women, we have got to learn that God needs us to completely be on board with His Plan for who we are. God made men a certain way and God made women a certain way. Once you accept that, you will learn that when we blur the lines of who we have been created to be, we have problems.

You may need to repeat this... get ready... "Men want to be Men!" (Repeat)

"Men wanted to be treated like Men." (Repeat)

"Men don't need to be reminded that you can take care of yourself and that you don't need their money!" (Repeat)

Men want to be respected! Money has nothing to do with that respect! We have to learn that we will not get what we are seeking by constantly being this self-sufficient woman who doesn't need anything or anyone. We need to understand that our strength is in our softness, or lovingness and our understanding. So many women assume that softness and lovingness equates to weakness and powerlessness. That is so far from truth! There is so much power in empowering your husband to be the leader in your home and or your family. The most powerful thing your husband can do for your children is to love you! When he shows your kids his love for you it will bring about a security that is so powerful, unlike anything you can imagine.

We must focus on how we can be better at being wives as God intended. The rewards are endless.

It's not the load that breaks you down, it's the way you carry it.
-Lena Horne

11

Sistas Doin' it for Themselves

———————

I get angry, upset, and argumentative when I hear people say that there are no good Black men. That's not true, and I am tired of that lie being perpetuated. Just because it's said over and over or even because that scenario fits the life of a person you know, doesn't make it true.

In addition, Black women who attribute being successful and strong as the reason why they are single and alone is equally untrue. What is likely, most women assume is that their success and credentials makes them attractive to the few good men out there.

Be proud that you have achieved big things on your job or in your career, but don't assume that because you have figured out how to be successful in the workplace, those same skills apply in relationships. Celebrate that you have overcome the odds and have enjoyed some semblance of success in your career—but the odds change when we look at love and marriage and you must learn to adjust. God is proud of you, and He wants you to be happy above all—but let us never assume that it is okay to abandon our core values in pursuit of a watered-down version of personal success when building strong relationships and stable families.

It feels good to beat the odds and become successful. There is nothing like climbing a corporate ladder, but there are other odds that are equally important to beat—and they are directly connected to your ability to be an amazing wife and mother. Why do we abandon this goal? It's funny how we can climb a corporate ladder, with every obstacle known to man—racism, sexism, lack of connections, non-Ivy League—You name it! Somehow, we have equated that success with the inability to build a successful marriage and happy family. It's the successful Black woman who is most prepared with resources, education, talent and the opportunity to be successful in family planning and marriage building. Somehow, the money and the power get in our way.

Let me introduce you to a young lady named Sandra. Our contact began in the early 1990s. She was a successful insurance agent who worked her way up the employment ladder. Soon she was at the corporate insurance company as director of cyber insurance and life was good. Sandra had been dating Carey since they were in their mid-twenties. He had a good job but lacked drive and ambition. Neither had kids and they were what many would have considered "great catches." Here is the problem. Carey never asked Sandra to get married; they were just "together." Sharing space in an apartment and allowing the years to roll by, Carey was with a woman that he felt didn't really need him and they didn't seem to notice the years as they slipped by.

Sandra and I began to communicate again in our early forties. I hadn't seen or heard from her in over twenty years. While doing research for this book, we reconnected again as I searched for successful women in my network to talk to about the issues that we are addressing. The woman I knew twenty years ago was gone. I struggled to hear her voice through the chaotic, unhinged barely coherent, broken thoughts and unfinished sentences that came from her mouth. It literally took me months to understand what happened to her because she never seemed to complete a thought while speaking. Finally, her story unfolded.

This strong woman was now a mother of one, a little girl. Carey was around, but they no longer were "together." After twenty years of existing in the same space, she had gone through a nervous breakdown, had been let go from the insurance company, and had completely gone through her savings and her 401k... all before age forty-five. How on earth could this happen?

Sandra never asked or required Carey to do anything because she was fine taking care of herself. At the beginning, that worked, but then "life" happened and she needed the support of a husband, not a man.

There are so many reasons why we feel there is no need to require much from the men we claim to love. This "low bar" or "few standards" approach to loving is a dangerous place to dwell long term. Everyone needs support and love. The very concept of marriage suggests that we are both all in together, but any man who would be okay with just being "together" is not a man you want in the first place. Remember, you set the standard... you create the environment. Any man will hang around—if you let him! Any man will never ask you to marry him if that's not what you have established that you want. Carey was perfectly fine just being there. Now that Sandra is older, she realizes she wasted so much time living in "limbo" with Carey—never requiring him to do anything but just be there... and that's exactly what he did, he was just—there.

Now that they have a child, she knows that he is not the example of a man she wants her daughter to see, but it's a bit too late for that. Now that she has a child, she sees that she wants more for herself than Carey—but at the same time, she doesn't want to deprive her daughter of her father... do you see where this is going? Do you see how our decisions create unique situations that can impact us for the rest of our lives?

I have heard it said so many times by countless women that, "He is a good man, but I really can do fine by myself!" Our desire make things "easy" and "less complicated" causes us to skip a few steps in our vetting process when it comes to the men we are with. We can't allow the fact that we can "take care of ourselves" hinder us from looking long and hard at who we are with. We can't allow ourselves to waste our good years in bad situations and then in our mature years blame the non-fact that there are limited or no men. When the truth will remain that your prime has past.

In other instances, we may find a great guy that may be totally into us and because it may seem to "good to be true," we want to separate our money from this man—requiring lifelong limited access to ensure that he is in it for love and not for the money (this always makes me laugh). Anytime we separate our money from our (potential) husband's money, we cut off access to what we hold of value. Separate money creates a dangerous atmosphere in a relationship.

This reminds me of another young lady I want to tell you about... her name is Victoria. Victoria is a beautiful family doctor who opened her practice in West Palm Beach back in the late 1990s. Single and full of life, her singleness seems a little unfair and soon you will understand.

Raised a Christian, with her mother and father at home, her parents constantly encouraged her to aim higher and constantly ask for more. She met a great guy named Jon. Jon was an engineering student, and they really enjoyed each other's company. When they met, she was in undergraduate school and he was had just started graduate school. Vickie's parents did everything in their power to discourage the relationship, which confused many folks because Vickie and Jon were a great match. They both believed the same things, their parents went to the same church, they complimented each other very well, but Vickie's mother felt that they were too young and she just thought there would be someone else more compatible.

Vickie and Jon split up for a few years, but they kept in touch. After medical school, Vickie reconnected with Jon and the passion was still there. Both in their late twenties, they were excited about getting back together, but Vickie's mother still felt there was someone better and she constantly discouraged the connection. By this time, Jon had a few setbacks in graduate school and was still working on his masters when Vickie's mother saw the opportunity to suggest that Vickie give him room to focus, so Vickie stepped back and didn't contact Jon as much. The problem that her family cited was, now that Vickie was a doctor and Jon appeared to be struggling, Vickie needed to find someone on her "level." Here was a couple who had survived almost ten years of being in school and apart, but they didn't have the support of family. In addition, the idea that Vickie was a doctor and Jon was still struggling with school was constantly injected as a red flag by her family.

As women, we have been wrongly taught to hold back things that we value out of an abundance of caution as it relates to men. Our caution or fears need to be tempered with prayer and an understanding of who we are and what we can accomplished where we are in life.

Here were two people who had survived a lot together, but her successes brought about caution and not excitement. Her successes could have been a major part of their survival, but, instead, after all that they had been through, Jon eventually met another woman and soon was married and has three children. Vickie on the other hand, is now about forty-three years old and a workaholic with no kids and no man in her life. She maintains that she will forever be in love with Jon. Even Jon speaks fondly of Vickie and feels that the opportunity just passed.

What happens when a woman meets a man that—although may not be where his woman is as it relates to success or education—loves her and feels comfortable with building a life with her? What we tend to forget is that life is more than just going to work and making money. There will be days where you will need a man to support you through a health challenge. There will be days when you will need a man you can trust. We often are willing to walk away from a man who loves us for one who is as educated as we are or makes more money than we do. I submit that our focus is all wrong. If you are looking to build an amazing family, love should be the first thing that you are looking to find in a partner—not a rich man.

The Evolution of Me

I told you about the day it hit me... you know, the day I realized that, though I made good money and I was successful, I didn't want to become a shell of a woman like the ladies I worked with on my job. That was the beginning. I identified that the culture that I was heavily involved with was not where I wanted to end up! I stopped caring about the money!

It was a few months later that I could truly get a handle on my issues. You see, I couldn't understand why I seemed doomed to be alone. I had the successful career, the Lexxus and the BMW, the rental property and the great condo in Hollywood, so why couldn't I get the guy and complete the package?

What was so wrong with me? I went to church. I volunteered. I did it all, but every guy was the same drama over and over again. Unlike most ladies, I stopped blaming the men. I stopped saying "all men are dogs" or that I was too much woman for these men. All of that was silliness to me and I didn't want to continue to perpetuate that lie to myself, making it even more difficult to truly break the chains that were holding me.

I blamed Satan himself... I did. Then I realized that I needed to stop blaming and look at me. Now before you put this book down with the intense side eye and teeth strip, hear me out.

I wanted to live like Claire Huxtable, but I sat down for hours watching the dysfunction of Meredith Grey, Derek Shepherd and Cristina Yang on *Grey's Anatomy*. I loved *Living Single* and *Friends*. All of them were shows that seemed harmless, fun and entertaining views of everyday life in Anywhere, USA. How could it be so bad to watch Kadesha and Rajean on *Living Single* constantly date and go through what seemed to be normal, daily, life experiences of the single woman. I used to love *Friends* too. Who could find anything wrong with a group of guys and gals living together, relying upon one another and just being there for one another.

We refuse to admit the influence of what we watch weekly. I was reminded of my personal evolution as I looked at my Facebook and Twitter feeds this week as I was writing this book. Everyone seems to be trending about the crazy dysfunction of Luscious and Cookie Lyons on *Empire*. The crazy mix bag of emotions that Olivia Pope seems to constantly be trapped in on *Scandal* and the heated edgy drama of *How to Get Away with Murder*. All these shows have sisters all around this country glued to their televisions—seemingly in love with the dysfunctional, trust lacking, insecure relationships they portray. Unable to find a real healthy relationship, women look to television to find something they can project their hopes and dreams upon.

We fail to realize how deeply connected what we see and what we attract can often be. When I watched *Friends* and *Living Single*, I found that I began to accept my singleness because I had an entertaining example of what my life had become. I didn't want to live with a bunch of girls, like on *Living Single*... sleeping with the occasional friend and constantly dating. I didn't want the *Friends* life either. Who wants to have all these great guy friends, but none of them are guys that are you are attracted to. Relationships seemed to elude the women in the examples that I just cited, and they were all okay with it.

Now, I am not advocating that something is wrong with being single. Not at all. I do believe, that when we seek God and prepare ourselves for the transformation from singleness to a lifelong partnership in marriage, there are somethings that will change—and loving foolishness, enjoying dysfunction and laughing at loneliness will not be your idea of entertainment once you have conclude that you are ready for real love.

The aforementioned shows are lightweight to the shows that are on today. I happened to catch a glimpse at what is currently on now while writing this book. I, like most, tuned into *Scandal* and *Empire* because I wanted to see the new shows and actors that seemed to be burning up the small screen and when I think of the mixed up dysfunctional craziness these shows dress up as entertaining, I realize there is no way that I could give an hour of my mind to such malarkey! Olivia Pope is in "love" with a married man that happens to be the president of the United States of America. It's not her fault she is in love with a man that can't get out of his marriage, right? In the same way, women all over this country find themselves in love with men who can't get out of their marriages, think about it!

When you come to the point in your experience where you are no longer entertained by such foolishness, then and only then will you realize it's the biggest trick of the Enemy to keep you constantly looking for dysfunction.

I knew I wanted a man who loved me and wanted heaven for me and the children that I bore for him. I knew I wanted a man who loved me and my mind, my dreams, my faults and imperfection. So why would I find Olivia Pope or Cookie Lyons entertaining and not repulsive? Why would I enjoy the constant sleeping around? What is so entertaining about *Desperate Housewives* of Atlanta, New York or Orange County?

When we are constantly witnessing dysfunction, we will breed dysfunction, whether you believe it or not. In the same way, would you go to a friend whose marriage is shaky for advice about how to find a man? Unless you feel that what she has is better than nothing at all, you will easily accept that as your only option and you will look to her for guidance. Now that sounds crazy, but we do it, because we have come to a point where we see dysfunction as reality.

Women are creatures of comradery. We crave relationships, and we look to relationships to help shape our views, our self-esteem and our future path. So many women aspire to be Olivia Pope. At least she found love, right? Unfortunately, it's with a man that will likely never, ever marry her.

When I was single, I finally concluded that I didn't want the crazy dysfunction that I witnessed on television. Once I made that decision, those shows were no longer entertaining to me. The same will happen for you. We have to want our healthy marriages and healthy lives more than the hour of craziness that we find so appealing. We truly are what we witness. We will attract what we find entertaining. It's very difficult to pray to Yahweh for a God-fearing husband who loves and respects you when you empathize with President Fitzgerald Grant and his unfortunate situation. There is no empathy when you have standards that Our Father in Heaven Himself has placed in your heart.

We must understand that when we respect the sanctity of marriage and hold it in high regard; we couldn't watch in enjoyment as any marriage unraveled. Who cares that it's not real! It doesn't matter! We must cherish the very concept of it. Our children need to know that when it's right, it's great—not crazy, violent or unreliable.

We must do better. We must seek a better understanding of what we are looking for... that's the only way we will attract better. When I came to this realization my evolution began. I changed and so did the people I attracted.

You're not obligated to win.
You're obligated to keep trying to
do the best you can every day.
-Marian Wright Edelman

12

This Whole Thing About Love and Respect

I know we can all recite the text together. Let do it, shall we: (throat clearing) Ephesians 25:22-25, 33

> *Wives, submit yourselves unto your own husbands, as unto the Lord. For the husband is the head of the wife, even as Christ is the head of the church: and he is the savior of the body. Therefore as the church is subject unto Christ, so let the wives be to their own husbands in everything. Husbands, love your wives, even as Christ also loved the church, and gave himself for it; But every husband must love his wife as he loves himself, and wives should respect their husbands.*

You know it's hard to respect a man you make more money than. Most men can't love a woman who doesn't respect him, at least not for long. So, when does the light bulb go off for most of the women reading this text? When will we realize that we measure our respect for a man by what he has instead of how he loves? I know I sound like a broken record on this, but I will say it again: YOU WILL NOT ALWAYS HAVE MONEY! On those days that you are broke, you need to respect the man you married and that love that he has for you will bring security that you will come to enjoy in your relationship.

Why can't women see it? Do we realize we are quick to love men that are clearly no good—but we struggle to respect a good man with no money? That's just how backwards we are! Until we realize our pattern, we will continually repeat it. Please, my sister, know this from a woman who was there. (Pull the book close, because I need you to get this.)

There is NO amount of money, no job, no car or house that can replace the love and adoration that I feel from my husband or my kids. When I think about all the blood sweat and tears that I put in my job and career and I compare it to my family—there is, like—NO COMPARISON! There is just something almost magical and beautiful about being where you belong. I know it's the biggest trick the enemy has ever waged on mankind to have our families upset like this. To have women choose to raise families alone and men making babies with every vagina willing to carry one! Women making great career moves and men struggling to find their place in all of it are a strategic attack! I see it now only because I didn't have a book like this fifteen years ago telling me what I am telling you now.

It is a trick! Think about it. Successful Black women are the most mentally ready women to have babies and change the direction of our children in this country but because of our choices and lack of mental and spiritual readiness, we usually find out in our late thirties and forties that health issues and advance maternal complications limit us to one or two children. Meanwhile, Shanenae—who is barely twenty, is having welfare babies left and right that will end up on government assistance for us all to pay for eventually!

Successful Black women are the most equipped to help change the educational direction of our families and the overall physical and spiritual health of our families. The reason why African American families are where they are is because we don't see the attack and we fall right in line with where the enemy would have us be—in our big ol' houses by ourselves, sipping tea, watching *Platinum Weddings* on WE TV!

The wisest of women builds
her house.
-Proverbs 14: 1

13

Where to Go From Here

———————

Now that you know what being a wife really is, you have got to decide whether or not you want that for yourself... meditate on it... internalize it and then pray! Not every woman will marry. If you want to get married, you need to understand the job description a whole lot better than you do. By understanding the job, it will affect where you submit applications!

We must come to grips with the fact that money alone will not secure our relationships. Your career and your degrees mean nothing in the light of heaven and the earthly home God will bless you with. There is a bigger picture. It's a delicate dance to find a way to transition from your career-minded agenda to one that is focused on supporting your husband while teaching and loving your kids. Most women outsource the husband and kids to someone or something else—thinking that it's okay to do that when it's not.

People call me old fashioned, but I don't care. My husband is the priest, head, leader—whatever you want to call him—of our home and family. That's the way God intended it to be and although he didn't feel comfortable at first with that position, it was my job to create the environment and to step back to allow him to see and explore the space that God designed for him.

Now that I am where I am, I feel more comfortable. Sure, I miss my corporate job and all the power it afforded me, but when I think about my sons—the young Black men that God has trusted me with, and when I think about how young Black men are viewed in our society—with all the traps and lures that the enemy has set for them... When I think about the Michael Browns and Trayvon Martins of this world who are gunned down in the street—I look to heaven and I tell my Father God and Creator that I will do my part!

"What is my part?" you may wonder. All of us have a part to play in strengthening our community so that we can stand together as families and communities—not as dysfunction and uninformed. There is no question that we are an amazing community when we are armed with informed, strong family units that are involved in the lives of our young people and make our political leaders accountable. When we are lost is when we are focused on ourselves. It's just not who we are as a people. We are a community that has always looked out for each other and our children. Even though we have been hit hard by the fragmented family units and the economic challenges that are often unique to our community, the Black Love that is often on display when we are strong and focused on our families is an undeniable force that empowers all of us. Have you ever seen some of the photos of Barack and Michelle Obama? Every time I see them, I just want to hug my husband. It also begs the question why some of the most racists individuals speak so heinously about her or them together. It's no question in my mind that there are many who are not use to Black Love, and they refuse to celebrate it. In the same way, it's no wonder we are not at a lost for Black Dysfunction in the media because that is more widely accepted as what is expected from our community.

I know one thing for sure; I will nurture this environment that we call home to ensure that my sons understand what is expected of them and what they are capable of. They must see their father as the head of our home and that he has the tools, the respect and the authority to be the leader of our family. We must focus on the way God intended our roles to be. Anything else will perpetuate the confusion that has made it so very difficult for the Black family to survive in America.

You must see that you, as a successful woman of color, are more qualified to build a family based on love and respect. Money is not an issue, and it won't be unless you make it one.

Who better to have a family than a woman like you—one with the resources and access to care that many women of color don't have.

Who better to be married than a woman like you—one who is educated and can devote time and resources into providing the education and training to empower Black boys and girls with the tools they need to be anything that they want to be?

Who better than you! You are articulate and exposed enough to know that you can build a legacy of love with a man that loves you back... a man that has a relationship with God and can discern the hidden darkness that plagues family after family trying to hold on.

We have to be honest with ourselves. The truth of it all rests with you. You are informed and capable on loving a man... not just any man, but the original man. Stop devaluing his worth, and understand that you hold the key to reevaluating his position in the world. You are the key to his success. We must do a better job of hold up the standard. Instead of lowering it to help a man that you shouldn't be with, why not elevate it to draw out the man that is looking for you.

About the Author

Carmen Hope Thomas was born in Ocala, FL in the early 1970s. Her childhood was split between Ocala and nearby Gainesville, Florida. Her mother, the late Carol Taylor Williams, was instrumental in helping Carmen strive for lofty heights. For example, in high school, Carmen won the Miss Talented Teen Florida—a pageant formed by famed radio personality Hal Jackson. Carmen won Miss Gainesville, Miss Florida and was recognized in the International Pageant at the Apollo Theater in New York as Miss Congeniality in 1990.

That experience paved the way for her being chosen to be Miss Oakwood College 1992 and being the first runner-up in the Miss Collegiate African American Pageant held at the MGM Studios in Orlando in 1993.

Carmen's career in radio began after graduation from Oakwood College—now Oakwood University—in 1994. She has been written about for her passions in newspaper articles both as a radio personality and as an actress. She stared in the stage play *Shakin' the Mess Outta Misery* in 1998 with director Desmond Walker, which opened the door for more acting opportunities.

In 1999, Carmen moved to Miami and worked at the renowned radio station WEDR FM, where she performed on air as a voice over artist and as an advertising manager.

In 2004, Carmen stepped out of radio to follow her passion for singing—releasing "Heaven" in 2005—even moving to the Washington, DC area. She toured the country singing and speaking for two years. Carmen got married in 2006 to Jason Thomas of Manchester, England and moved from Washington, DC back to Miami, FL. For almost two years, Carmen and Jason lived between Miami and Panama City, Panama. After the birth of their first child, they lived in Miami where Carmen got involved with many projects. She started the "Magdela House"—a placement program for battered women. Her passion for the program was pivotal in helping many women and children become safe.

Carmen had a string of health challenges that allowed her to reflect on her relationship with God and her family. Now, a mother of two, and after being married for almost ten years, her focus is on the future. She has helped her husband, Jason—who is a financial coach, create Future Family Finance, a business that helps teach families how to pass wealth to the next generation.

Carmen and Jason travel the country doing Husband and Wife Financial Bootcamps, and they have both authored the Finance Manual—"Mind Over Money." Through her travels, Carmen has held single women forums, which have allowed her to speak directly to the cries of women who are successful and single, something she herself can relate too. It's through these forums that she has heard the complex issues successful women, especially women of color, are having finding and enjoying loving relationships. It's through her own struggles and successes that she began to document her thoughts and author this book.

Carmen lives with her family in Northern Alabama, and they are very happy.

*****

Contact Carmen for Book Signings at:
Booking@CarmenHopeThomas.com

Quotes Database

1. "Behold, you are beautiful, my love, behold, you are beautiful! Your eyes are doves behind your veil." -Song of Solomon 4:1
2. "She opens her hand to the poor and reaches out her hands to the needy." -Proverbs 31:20
3. "A gracious woman gets honor." -Proverbs 11:16
4. "It is better to live in a desert land than with a quarrelsome and fretful woman." -Proverbs 21:19
5. "It is true that a fellow cannot ignore women- but he can think of them as he ought- as sisters, not as sparring partners." -Jim Elliot
6. "If you don't like something, change it. If you can't change it, change your attitude." -Maya Angelou
7. "Trust yourself. Think for yourself. Act for yourself. Speak for yourself. Be yourself. Imitation is suicide." -Marva Collins
8. "Once we recognize what it is we are feeling, once we recognize we can feel deeply, love deeply, can feel joy, then we will demand that all parts of our lives produce that kind of joy." –Audre Lorde

9. "Whatever someone did to you in the past has no power over the present. Only you give it power." -Oprah Winfrey

10. "You may encounter many defeats, but you must not be defeated. In fact, it may be necessary to encounter the defeats, so you can know who you are, what you can rise from, how you can still come out of it." -Maya Angelou

11. "Think like a queen. A queen is not afraid to fail. Failure is another steppingstone to greatness." -Oprah Winfrey

12. "It's time for you to move, realizing that the thing you are seeking is also seeking you." -Iyanla Vanzant

13. "You are on the eve of a complete victory. You can't go wrong. The world is behind you." –Josephine Baker

14. "The triumph can't be had without the struggle." –Wilma Rudolph

15. "We will be ourselves and free, or die in the attempt. Harriet Tubman was not our great-grandmother for nothing." -Alice Walker

16. "'I can't' are two words that have never been in my vocabulary. I believe in me more than anything in this world." -Wilma Rudolph

17. "Someone was hurt before you, wronged before you, hungry before you, frightened before you, beaten before you, humiliated before you, raped before you...yet, someone survived...You can do anything you choose to do." -Maya Angelou

18. "When I dare to be powerful – to use my strength in the service of my vision, then it becomes less and less important whether I am afraid. " -Audre Lorde

19. When there is no enemy within, the enemies outside cannot hurt you." -African Proverb

20. "Whatever you fear most has no power – it is your fear that has the power. The thing itself cannot touch you. But if you allow your fear to seep into your mind and overtake your thoughts, it will rob you of your life." -Oprah Winfrey

21. "I have learned over the years that when one's mind is made up, this diminishes fear; knowing what must be done does away with fear." -Rosa Parks

22. "I used to want the words 'She tried' on my tombstone. Now I want 'She did it.'" -Katherine Dunham

23. "Success doesn't come to you...you go to it." -Marva Collins

24. "Whatever we believe about ourselves and our ability comes true for us." -Susan L. Taylor

25. "Nothing will work unless you do." -Maya Angelou

26. "Ask for what you want and be prepared to get it." -Maya Angelou

27. "We are all gifted. That is our inheritance." -Ethel Waters

28. "Success is liking yourself, liking what you do, and liking how you do it." -Maya Angelou

Citations

1. Beamon, Nika C. *I Didn't Work This Hard Just to Get Married: Successful Single Black Women Speak out*. Chicago: Lawrence Hill, 2009. Print.

2. Harvey, Jill Rhodes. "SUCCESSFUL Women Don't Attract HUSBANDS..but Why!" *HubPages*. HubPages, n.d. Web. 02 Dec. 2016.

3. Holbrook, Karen. "Statistics Mask the Real Story of Women in Higher Education." *The New York Times*. N.p., n.d. Web.

4. "U.S. Bureau of Labor Statistics." *U.S. Bureau of Labor Statistics*. U.S. Bureau of Labor Statistics, n.d. Web. 2016.

5. "U.S. Bureau of Labor Statistics." *U.S. Bureau of Labor Statistics*. U.S. Bureau of Labor Statistics, n.d. Web. 02 Dec. 2016.

6. "U.S. Bureau of Labor Statistics." *U.S. Bureau of Labor Statistics*. U.S. Bureau of Labor Statistics, n.d. Web. 02 Dec. 2016.

7. "The Journal of Blacks in Higher Education." *The Journal of Blacks in Higher Education*. N.p., n.d. Web. 02 Dec. 2016.

8. Klotz, Frieda. "Is Marriage Still Worth It." *Forbes*. Forbes Magazine, 8 Feb. 2012. Web. 02 Dec. 2016.

9. Gottlieb, Lori. "Settling for Mr. Good Enough." *The Atlantic*. Atlantic Media Company, Mar. 2008. Web. 02 Dec. 2016.

10. Bolick, Kate. "All the Single Ladies." *The Atlantic*. Atlantic Media Company, Nov. 2011. Web. 02 Dec. 2016.

11. Karol, Gabrielle. "This Is Why More Black Women Aren't Getting Married." *Business Insider*. Business Insider, 21 Feb. 2012. Web. 02 Dec. 2016.

12. Dredge, Stuart. "42% of People Using Dating App Tinder Already Have a Partner, Claims Report." *The Guardian*. Guardian News and Media, 07 May 2015. Web. 02 Dec. 2016.

13. "The Journal of Blacks in Higher Education." *The Journal of Blacks in Higher Education*. N.p., n.d. Web. 02 Dec. 2016.

14. "Bar and Bat Mitzvah." *Wikipedia*. Wikimedia Foundation, n.d. Web. 02 Dec. 2016.

15. "Rite of Passage." *Wikipedia*. Wikimedia Foundation, 5 June 2008. Web. 02 Dec. 2016.

16. "The Journal of Blacks in Higher Education." *The Journal of Blacks in Higher Education*. N.p., n.d. Web. 02 Dec. 2016.

17. "Population." *BlackDemographics.com*. N.p., 8 Sept. 2012. Web. 02 Dec. 2016.

18. "Population." *BlackDemographics.com*. N.p., 8 Sept. 2012. Web. 02 Dec. 2016.

19. "April | 2011 | DESANews – United Nations Department of Economic and Social Affairs." *United Nations*. United Nations, Aug. 2011. Web. 02 Dec. 2016.

20. Cadet, Danielle. "5 Lies We Should Stop Telling About Black Fatherhood." *The Huffington Post*. TheHuffingtonPost.com, 13 June 2014. Web. 02 Dec. 2016.

21. COATES, TA-NEHISI. *The Atlantic*. Atlantic Media Company, 21 June 2013. Web. 02 Dec. 2016.